"Arlene Pellicane knows exactly wh[...]lappy *Husband* is a delightful, entertaini[...]p to your husband's heart. The day it is rel[...], I'm putting it in my wife's hands!"

—David Clarke, marriage seminar speaker and author of
Kiss Me Like You Mean It and *I Don't Love You Anymore*

"A meaningful read for any wife who wants to get closer to her husband."

—David Jeremiah, bestselling author, pastor,
and founder of Turning Point Ministries

"As a woman who has been married for 40 years (obviously a *very* young bride), I plan to have just as much fun, if not more, in the next 40. *31 Days to a Happy Husband* is going to help make that happen. I thank you, Arlene, and so does my hubby, John!"

—Kendra Smiley, speaker and author of bestselling
Journey of a Strong-Willed Child (coauthored with her happy husband)

"When it comes to loving our husbands, most of us need more than a pep talk—we need a coach who understands where we're coming from and how to get us to that sweet God-spot in our relationship. Well, meet Coach Arlene. She's been there, done that in her marriage and will give you not just the steps but the motivation to take your marriage from roommates to making room for the most important man in your life."

—Kathi Lipp, national speaker and author of *The Husband Project*

"Here's fresh help and hope from popular author and speaker Arlene Pellicane. You'll find wisdom that works and new ideas that challenge you to stretch and grow. Arlene points the way to a happier, healthier marriage relationship—starting from right where you are today. An excellent, well-organized resource for wives!"

—David Frisbie, executive director, The Center for Marriage
and Family Studies, Del Mar, California

"We believe in the great advice in *31 Days to a Happy Husband* because we know Arlene and her husband, James—and he is happy! Arlene is always practical and personal, so this book is likely to make your husband very happy you bought it."

—Bill and Pam Farrel, authors of *Red-Hot Monogamy* and
Men Are Like Waffles—Women Are Like Spaghetti

"Wives ask us all the time, 'How can I encourage my husband to grow and change? How can I help him become the man God calls him to be?' As Arlene wisely reminds us here, the answer is not more nagging or more begging. Instead, we can use our God-given role as wives to support, nurture, and respect our husbands—watching as God works through our open and available hearts. I am glad to recommend Arlene's new books to wives of all ages!"

—Lisa Frisbie, author of *Becoming Your Husband's Best Friend*

"*31 Days to a Happy Husband* gives every wife the tools she needs to have a joyful home. You'll learn how to set biblical priorities that may save your marriage or change the dynamic of your relationship from good to great. Arlene shares her own experiences along with expert advice from many happy husbands to help you have a happy husband yourself!"

—Beverly LaHaye, founder, Concerned Women for America and bestselling author of *The Act of Marriage*

"Sound, practical wisdom for any wife who wants to bless her husband and be the wife God has called her to be."

—Bob Lepine, cohost, *FamilyLife Today*

"What a delightful book! With her touching stories, biblical insights, and practical helps, Arlene Pellicane walks you through a fun yet meaningful adventure of investing in your husband's happiness and ultimately, yours. Enjoy the read, as well as the rewards!"

—Cindi McMenamin, author of *When a Woman Inspires Her Husband* and *When Couples Walk Together*

"If you're going to talk about a happy husband—and a happy wife—you have to talk about a mutually fulfilling sex life. Arlene's book helps you identify roadblocks to intimacy while discovering true passion. No doubt you will benefit from this 31-day journey to greater joy inside and outside the bedroom."

—Clifford and Joyce Penner, authors of *The Gift of Sex*

to a Happy Husband

31 Days

Arlene Pellicane

HARVEST HOUSE PUBLISHERS
EUGENE, OREGON

Cover design by Left Coast Design, Portland, Oregon

Cover photo © Yuri Arcurs / Shutterstock

31 DAYS TO A HAPPY HUSBAND
Copyright © 2012 by Arlene Pellicane
Published by Harvest House Publishers
Eugene, Oregon 97402
www.harvesthousepublishers.com

Library of Congress Cataloging-in-Publication Data
    Pellicane, Arlene, 1971-
    31 days to a happy husband / Arlene Pellicane.
       p. cm.
    ISBN 978-0-7369-4632-2 (pbk.)
    ISBN 978-0-7369-4633-9 (eBook)
    1. Marriage—Religious aspects—Christianity. 2. Husbands—Psychology. 3. Wives—
Conduct of life. I. Title. II. Title: Thirty-one days to a happy husband.
    BV835.P45 2012
    248.8'435—dc23
                                                                        2011043749

Printed in the United States of America.

12 13 14 15 16 17 18 19 20 / BP-SK / 10 9 8 7 6 5 4 3 2

For James
The keeper of the flame

Contents

Are You Still Dreaming?

The year was 1999 and my big moment had finally arrived. I stood holding my father's arm, ready to make my grand entrance into the church. James and I had decided to have one of his favorite seminary professors marry us. Ours was only his second wedding to officiate, but we didn't care about his inexperience.

Just as I approached the door leading into the sanctuary, I was shocked to hear the sound of our professor's voice, "Dearly beloved, we are gathered here to bring James and Arlene together in holy matrimony." The only problem was, I was still standing in the hall with all the bridesmaids. Our professor mistook a break in the music as his cue to begin the ceremony.

I couldn't believe my eyes or ears. Our dear professor got all the way through his introduction before realizing his error. When he got to that famous line, "Who gives this woman to be married to this man?" there was complete silence. Our friends and family didn't know whether to laugh or be mortified.

At this, my aunt started playing the piano, and I was thrust through the door of the church to join my ceremony *in progress*. I never thought in my wildest dreams that I'd miss the beginning of my own wedding, but it sure has given us many laughs over the years.

Do you remember the day you said "I do"? I hope the ceremony didn't start without you. Remember walking down the aisle, feeling like the happiest woman in the world? Your heart was full of dreams for the future. Are you still dreaming today?

Keep Honeymooning

So many couples told us after we tied the knot, "Just wait until you've been married a few years. You won't be so lovey-dovey anymore." But there was one lone voice who gave us the opposite advice. "Never let the honeymoon end," he said. "It's much easier to keep love alive than to try to revive something that has died." We vowed to follow his advice.

Fast-forward the tape twelve years to our aha moment. James and I were teaching a young-marrieds class at our church. On the first day of class, we noticed there was not a centimeter of space in between these newlywed couples. Wives were superglued to their husbands' sides. Eyes were locked, hands were held, hair was twirled. I looked over at my James who was sitting about a foot away from me. We, the sage teachers, needed a refresher course on touch, affection, and romance.

Most likely you know what I'm talking about. The heat of passion turns into the warmth of companionship. But that warmth, if we don't take time to stoke the embers, can slowly turn into a cool disengagement between husband and wife. And before you know it, you're two roommates sharing a home, a bank account, and children.

I don't want that dull fate and neither do you. Three kids later and in our forties, James and I are learning to flirt again. The good news is you can relearn how to do all the things you used to do when you were dating. Except that instead of being lovers on cruise control, you might have to step on the gas pedal once in a while for the ride of your life.

Time to Dream Again

I remember driving down the freeway and seeing a pickup truck with these bold words printed on the back window: "Happy to be here, proud to serve." I'd like you to imagine those words hanging in a frequented place in your home. When you can say about your home, "Happy to be here and proud to serve," your husband will want to hurry home every day because it's the place he feels most valued and loved.

This book will help you create that kind of place for your man. It's divided into thirty-one daily readings grouped into five simple sections that will help you demonstrate to your husband the love that hooked him in the first place. The titles for each section form the acrostic DREAM. After all, the marriage of your dreams doesn't have to be a fairy tale that will never come true. You can experience the kind of marriage most people dream about by following these five guidelines:

> **D**= *Domestic Tranquillity*—Your husband needs a peaceful haven (Days 1-5).

> **R** = *Respect*—Your husband needs to be honored in his own home (Days 6-11).

> **E** = *Eros*—Your husband needs a fulfilling sex life (Days 12-19).

> **A** = *Attraction*—Your husband needs to be attracted to you (Days 20-26).

> **M**= *Mutual Activities*—Your husband needs to have fun with you (Days 27-31).

Ask any husband if he would be happy having these five things in greater measure, and I can assure you his answer will be a resounding yes! And you just might find yourself enjoying these things too.

Notice Him, Nurture Him

It doesn't take much time or effort to see that our culture is pessimistic about marriage. A happy marriage seems more like a fairy tale that Pollyanna dreamed up fifty years ago. Today's wives are complaining left and right about their husbands' many shortcomings. In fact, many women would never pick up a book like this. Why should a wife make her *husband* happy when he's not making *her* happy? I like what host Bob Lepine of *Family Life Today* says, "Our role is not to figure out how to fix our spouse. Our role is: How do we reflect Christ in the marriage?"[1]

And check out this insight from one husband:

> When a woman is engaged to be married, she pours all her nurture into her man. She holds him, kisses him, and talks sweetly to him. They have fun together, do interesting things together, and enjoy the physical affection of first love. Then after they marry and have kids, all that nurture that went originally to the husband is suddenly transferred to the children. The kids benefit from all the maternal instincts and become the primary focus of all her tender nurture. The husband is just as needy for that nurture, but he is too proud to admit it.

When you look at your husband, you're probably thinking he looks pretty self-sufficient. The other people in your life vying for your attention are truly needy (your children, grandchildren, aging parent, depressed friend). Look again. Your husband craves your affection and care but doesn't want to ask for it. He bites the bullet because he's supposed to be the strong one. Yet he desperately wants tender loving care just as you do.

How to Get the Most Out of This Book

The thirty-one happy husbands I interviewed for this book will serve as your insider guides for the next thirty-one days. Here are a few suggestions for how best to glean their insights as you read through this book:

Commit to reading a chapter every day for one month. Choose a month to soak your husband in tender loving care. Maybe choose his birthday month or your anniversary month to make it extra special and more memorable. But don't worry—if you want to start today and his birthday isn't for months, I'm sure he won't mind! If you fall behind one or two days, don't give up on the "Happy Husband" month. The chapters are short so you can easily catch up and get back on track.

Read it in five chunks. Maybe you want to tackle more than one day's reading at a time. Once you're settled in your comfortable chair to read, you want to keep going. Then I suggest you divide your reading into sections. Begin with Days 1-5, which cover Domestic Tranquillity. This way you can concentrate your focus on one key DREAM factor at a time. After you've completed the action steps suggested, you can move on to the letter *R* for Respect (Days 6-11), and so on.

Read the affirmation for happy wives aloud once a day. You'll find this daily affirmation on page 179. Put your affirmation on your bathroom mirror and read it out loud every morning. Expect to feel uncomfortable doing this at first. But after a few days, not only will you believe the words you are saying, you will be living them out. It's tempting to skip this step, so when you're done reading today, turn to page 179. Photocopy, scan, or type out the page and put it on your bathroom mirror tonight.

Start a "Wives of Happy Husbands Discussion Group." Read the book together with a group of friends who also want to add some sizzle to their marriages. Use the discussion guide on pages 185-192. Plan to meet weekly for five weeks to discuss what you're learning. I promise these will be lively coffee dates or meals together!

Do the action steps. If you just read the book without trying any of the action steps, your husband probably won't be able to tell you're reading a book about how to love him better. At the end of each day's reading, you'll find these two recurring themes:

- *Notice Today*—You'll be invited to take a close look at your husband. It will take only a few moments, but it will make a big difference. When you notice something positive about your husband instead of taking him for granted or rehearsing his faults, you'll experience a change of heart and greater warmth for your man.

- *Nurture Today*—You'll get to put your attitude into action through the daily steps to nurture him. Remember, if you don't *do* anything differently this month toward your spouse, your thirty-one-day journey to marital bliss isn't much more than wishful thinking.

Every day of your life, you're either building your husband up or tearing him down. Proverbs 14:1 says, "The wise woman builds her house, but with her own hands the foolish one tears hers down." In the next thirty-one days, you're going to launch a full-force, no-holding-back, life-changing building program for your marriage. Let other things slide while you make your husband the number one priority for the next thirty-one days. Your only agenda is to overwhelm him with attention and affirmation.

Roll up your sleeves. It's time to build and dream again.

Do You Have a Happy Husband?

Before you begin reading Day 1, take this self-assessment to discover what areas in your marriage need the most attention. Be honest in your answers. You're not trying to impress anyone here. Your goal is to gain valuable insight about your husband's current level of happiness in your marriage.

1. The environment of my home is warm and peaceful on most days.

   ❏ Yes   ❏ No

2. I drop other things (even with my kids) to make time for my husband if he needs anything.

   ❏ Yes   ❏ No

3. I never say unkind things about my husband to others.

   ❏ Yes   ❏ No

4. If there's a decision to be made, my husband has the final say.

   ❏ Yes   ❏ No

5. I enjoy having sex and look forward to making love to my husband.

   ❏ Yes   ❏ No

6. My husband and I talk regularly about ways to improve our sex life.

   ❑ Yes   ❑ No

7. I make an effort to look attractive with my clothes, hair, and makeup even on days when I see only my husband.

   ❑ Yes   ❑ No

8. I am a healthy body weight and exercise at least three times a week.

   ❑ Yes   ❑ No

9. My husband and I go on a date at least once a month.

   ❑ Yes   ❑ No

10. We still enjoy romance, kissing once a day for at least five seconds.

   ❑ Yes   ❑ No

Total the number of yes answers:

1-4: Your relationship is on shaky ground. There are some critical areas of unmet needs that you must identify both for yourself and your husband. Reading this book is perfect timing.

5-7: You have some good habits and attitudes to build on. As you make a few key changes this month, you and your husband will be laughing, flirting, and enjoying each other's company more.

8-10: You have a happy husband. By the time you finish reading this book, he will be ecstatic. You'll be moving from good to great (or great to unbelievable). Be on the lookout for other women to encourage and mentor along the way.

Domestic Tranquillity
Your husband needs a peaceful haven.

Respect

Eros

Attraction

Mutual Activities

From Chaos to Calm

"If a house is divided against itself,
that house cannot stand."

MARK 3:25

When I heard that CHAOS stood for "Can't Have Anyone Over Syndrome," I could relate. I can't completely blame my two-, five-, and seven-year-old for the mess, but they certainly contribute to the clutter factor in my home. Don't get me wrong. I'm no Martha Stewart. My idea of a home-cooked meal is grilled chicken, broccoli, and rice. That's pretty much three ingredients *total*.

You won't catch me doing linens on Mondays, mopping on Wednesdays, and cleaning the blinds every other Friday. One fine day, I was actually cleaning the blinds downstairs. James, alarmed that the kids might be messing with something fragile, yelled down from upstairs, "What's that noise?"

"It's me, cleaning the blinds," I yelled back.

He was speechless for a few moments and then said, "We've been married twelve years, and I've *never* heard you clean the blinds."

I'm still full of surprises.

The Invasion

James was listening to radio-show host Dennis Prager as he talked about the average home with kids in America. Take a peek into that home and you'll most likely find the kids have taken over the establishment. Prager recalled that in generations past, kids had their toys exclusively in their rooms. The living room, dining room, kitchen, and master bedroom looked like rooms adults lived in. Today the tables have turned. Parents trip over trucks and dolls in every room of the house.

As James shared all this, my heart began to pound faster. I knew what was coming next. I can blame my mean, toy-intolerant husband, but the thought was actually springing from my own heart too. *Our house really needs an overhaul*...and so it began.

The next morning, I took a pad of paper and walked around the house with my kids. "Let's count how many rooms we have in the house and how many of those rooms have your toys in it," I said cheerfully as if this was going to be fun. We counted the living room, family room, loft, master bedroom, kids' bedrooms, and storage room and recorded that there were toys in *every* room of the house. I gave my lecture about how Mommy and Daddy owned the house and needed to have toy-free zones.

Saturday morning, we moved toys into the kids' rooms and filled up four bags for charity. For the first time in years, we sat in an uncluttered living room. Wow, that felt good. Now I'm not half as nervous about someone dropping by the house unexpectedly.

When the kids and I pitched in to declutter the house, what do you think that communicated to my husband? *You can voice your needs, and we will do our best to rise to the challenge.* It could have easily gone the other direction. *That's nice that you heard that inspiring radio program, but it is impossible to get these kids to organize their toys.* Guess what? It feels really good to do the right thing to bless your spouse.

You may not have children in the house, but you know clutter. Whether it's a tower of magazines and catalogs, art and sewing projects, or product samples for your home business, ask if your husband finds the house a tranquil place. Don't defend yourself, just listen.

Visible Calm

After a man has battled it out at work all day, you can imagine how nice it is to walk into a neat and welcoming home. For mothers of young children, *reasonably* neat does just fine. When Southern California radio host Roger Hedgecock comes home, he would like the table set, appetizer out, and a warm greeting from his wife, Cindy. Music is optional. Then he takes a few minutes alone to decompress from three hours of live talk radio. Cindy has learned to give him that space, and then they have a great evening together.[1]

Do you think it's too much for a husband to ask for a kiss hello and a table set for dinner? Too many American families have bought the lie that an evening meal together is a thing of the past. A peaceful home is impossible if children have anything to do with it. The impeccable and gracious June Cleaver of the classic *Leave It to Beaver* TV show is yesterday's reality. Nowadays, it's fast food in the minivan or frozen dinners around the tube.

There's no need to wear a string of pearls or dress up like June Cleaver, but that doesn't mean you can't welcome your hubby home with a smile and food. The meal may simply be a rotisserie chicken and salad bought from the store, but at least it's not served in a paper wrapper or Styrofoam box. I like what my friend Lori, mother of five, says: "It doesn't always work out, but on most days, I have the house picked up and the dinner ready." Don't strive for perfection. Shoot for *most days*.

If you have young children as I do, you can teach them how to set the table and the drill for cleaning toys off the floor before Daddy comes home. My friend Beth, mother of four, asks her husband to call her before coming home so she can get the kids cleaning up. She found out quickly that a five-minute warning wasn't nearly enough, so her husband has to call at least fifteen minutes in advance if he wants the house to be in order. My husband has a favorite verse to quote in the kitchen to the kids: "If anyone will not work, neither shall he eat" (2 Thessalonians 3:10 NKJV).

Overwhelmed at the thought of straightening the house before your husband's arrival? Start small but start somewhere. If all you can do is clear a path between the garage door and his chair at the dinner table, so be it. Once that's a no-brainer, pick another area of the house to straighten up before his arrival.

If you're a working mom, you may be rushing into the house at the same time your husband arrives or later. Twice-a-month cooking may be the answer to that dreaded question, "What's for dinner?" There are a variety of cookbooks available with doable plans to cook several meals in one day, freezing the majority of the meals to enjoy later.[2] I have found the hours spent slaving in the kitchen are actually worth the reward of coming home and enjoying a homemade meal with TV-dinner simplicity.

Invisible Calm

Even more important than a neat home and a hot meal is a warm welcome. Your home can be neat as a pin, but if you're cold toward your mate, he might as well live in an igloo in the Arctic. But what if you've had a lousy day? I know I've had bad mornings and still managed to smile at a room full of strangers in a meeting. Somehow we can put negative feelings behind us and act civilly—even warmly—to friends and acquaintances. Yet our spouse gets the emotional scraps of the day.

Why not pay the same respect to your best friend, your spouse, that you would give your boss or acquaintance? You say, "But that's fake. I want to be real with my spouse." Well, if your spouse was real with you all the time, he'd come home most days fuming, stressing, and fussing about the nonsense he endured at work. It's one thing to commiserate together over a bad day. It's another thing to bring your crabbiness, worry, anxiety, and irritation to the dinner table.

The Bible says it exactly this way twice, "Better to live on a corner of the roof than share a house with a quarrelsome wife" (Proverbs 21:9; 25:24). The writer of this proverb would rather live in a cheerless spot exposed to the elements than in a comfortable house with a sour, scolding woman. No external conveniences can replace the desire and need for internal peace.

John Fuller, host of *Focus on the Family* and father of six, says,

> A spick-and-span home and a wife who's on top of everything may be secondary to more important things like: What's the tone of the home? What's the character that we're working on? What's the sense of the Holy Spirit's presence here? I don't want to be in a pristine home that doesn't have God at the heart of it.[3]

The invisible calm John's wife, Dena, provides strengthens him day in and day out. A reservoir of joy even after a trying day is possible because of Jesus Christ. More important than a decluttered entryway and tasty dinner is the invisible calm your attitude creates.

Notice Today:

Imagine the challenges your husband faces at work this week. Any deadlines coming up or strained relationships with coworkers? Is he unemployed, underemployed, or overemployed right now? How would you rate his stress level?

Nurture Today:

When your husband walks in the door today, greet him with a warm smile, a hug, and a kiss that lasts at least five seconds. Straighten up the house a few minutes before his arrival.

Super Daddy

"Honor your father…"
EXODUS 20:12

My husband doesn't get it when women gush over the beauty of a newborn baby. Cupid's arrow missed him even when our first child was born. He thought that hairy seven-pounder looked like a monkey. Even if some men say about seeing their newborns, "It was love at first sight," James tells me many men don't relate. At the beginning, it's more like, "Does this lump come with instructions?"

Digital Shepherds founder Tshaka Armstrong recalls changing his baby girl's first diaper at the hospital. As he changed the diaper, his wife gasped in horror. "What are you doing? You don't wipe from back to front. You wipe from front to back." As his wife was going ballistic on him, he looked calmly at her and said, "We have different plumbing. I never have to worry about which direction I wipe."[4]

Just because a man has to *learn* about the right direction to wipe or how to take care of a seven-pound lump doesn't mean he can't do it well. Sometimes we start on the wrong foot from Day 1 of parenting, assigning ourselves "Queen Mother Know-It-All" and our husbands "Dunce-Cap Daddy." How can a man prove he's a capable father if his wife criticizes his every move and constantly compares his methods with hers? After a while, he will stop trying. Disengaged, he'll earn the new degrading title "Deadbeat Dad."

If someone asked your husband, "How would your wife rate you as a father?" what do you think he would say? Super Daddy? Decent Daddy? Flawed-But-Trying Daddy? Lame Daddy?

Wives, we have incredible power to shape our husband's belief about how effective he is as a father. Do we verbally praise him when he shoots hoops with the kids, follows through on a promise, and doles out discipline? Do we bite our tongue when he throws all the kids' laundry in at once—darks, whites, delicates, and beach towels? Do we raise our eyebrows and mutter under our breath when he suggests a family activity we think is a bad idea? We may cheer our husbands on as fathers in our hearts, but day to day, what are we communicating to him? Sometimes we're tearing down his "father esteem," totally unaware of what we are doing.

Oatmeal at 10:00

Several years ago, I returned home from a women's ministry event at church. I pulled into my driveway around 10:00 p.m., certain my one-year-old Ethan would be fast asleep in his cozy crib. Imagine my surprise when I opened the garage door to find James's car missing. A few minutes later, here comes James, strolling in with baby Ethan. He had taken Ethan to the mall to look for an iPod (for James, not for Ethan). I was ticked. And now Ethan needed to be fed oatmeal because he was hungry. *At ten o'clock at night.*

My mind whirled and my face grew hot with anger. The dishes were piled high in the sink; Ethan was in his high chair eating oatmeal. *Can't you just get him to bed at a decent hour and do the dishes?* I thought as I glared at the supposedly responsible party. James was cool as a cucumber and actually made me feel like the foolish one. "Lighten up. One night won't kill him."

Later (and I mean a few years later) I realized something about that night. Instead of being so indignant, I could have come home grateful. I could have chosen to say, "Thank you for watching Ethan for the last five hours so I could go to a women's event and get recharged." I could have said, "Not many men would gladly watch their one-year-old and even dare to take them to the mall, but I guess you guys had a great time." Our husbands may not enforce the crib curfew like we do, but our children are still living and breathing aren't they? I'm thinking now that James was right. One night on the town didn't kill my baby.

Put Yourself in His Shoes

Remember Tshaka changing his baby's diaper and wiping the wrong direction? From his perspective, he wasn't doing anything wrong. He was getting the job done as best he knew how. He wasn't maliciously thinking, *Let me be lazy and wipe all crazy so my baby can get some kind of infection.* We can see that clearly about Tshaka, but when it's our own husband doing something we perceive as wrong, that's another story.

I remember the night before Mother's Day in 2008. I wanted a low-key evening of cleaning the kitchen, getting the kids bathed, and calling it a night. But James was itching to go out, and some friends invited us over. He eagerly accepted. It was the first spontaneous thing we had done in months. I really did enjoy myself, but when 9:00 rolled around and my husband was still yakking, it went south for me. By the time we got into the car, I'm stewing. *Tomorrow is Mother's Day. It's so unfair that I still have a pile of dishes to do when we get home. My husband is selfish. I wanted to go home an hour ago for the kids, but we had to stay because he's having a good time. Doesn't he know the children have to go to sleep?*

After finally putting the kids to bed, I'm pouting and spouting, "I still have to wrap my gift for my mom and do the dishes." He simply answers, "At least we had a great time," which of course makes me madder and furthers my "he is so selfish" storyline.

In my frustration, I took a breath and tried to picture what this evening had looked like from my husband's perspective. He had asked me if we had plans, and I had said no. He accepted our friend's invitation to dinner, and there was nothing wrong with that. We stayed out an extra hour, but that wasn't really a big deal. Our kids had a great time (they got to watch *Cars*), so why was I bent out of shape? It dawned on me that all my huffing and puffing was robbing him of the joy of finally doing something spontaneous. Since I'm a planner with small kids, we don't do spontaneous. When I walked through the evening in his shoes, I saw that he hadn't done a terrible thing to sabotage my Mother's Day or injure the kids. He was just trying to have a nice evening. Perhaps it was *me* who was being selfish. Ouch.

Your husband is bound to do something with your kids that displeases you. I'm not talking about moral matters that must be hammered out; I'm talking about style. He may throw your kids in the air too high, wrestle too rough, and keep them out too late. Put yourself in his shoes. Vow to see things from his perspective, and you'll find yourself cutting him the slack he desperately needs.

Gimme an S

You would think from my stories that James has no respect for our kids' bedtimes, but that isn't true. In all fairness, I've got to show you the other side of the coin. Right now as I write, James has all the kids out of the house for me. Pretty much all the things I can do as a parent, he can do better and faster. When the kids are sick, James is the doctor of the house and takes the night shift. As a realtor, he sets his schedule so most days he can bike with Ethan to and from his elementary school. He's the choco-late-chip-cookie baker, piano teacher, and Lego maker. I'm married to a Super Daddy, and guess what? You probably are too. You just have to look for the *S* on his chest.

What are things your husband does well with your kids? You get more of what you measure. If you notice and praise the positives in your hus-band's parenting, you'll get the good stuff from him in spades. Author and family counselor David Frisbie says,

> Men like to feel successful. If they come home and get a laun-dry list of what they haven't done, or what they need to be doing, or what they should be doing—"Why don't you ever help with this?" or "Why aren't you doing that?" or "I told you about this three weeks ago"—no wonder there's some urgent project at work. They need to come home to an environment where they are seen as successes and where they feel successful as a dad. I would say positive reinforcement way past the saccharin point where you can't stand it anymore. If you get to the saccharin and you can't stand it, you're on your way. Keep going. Men need a lot of positive reinforcement.[5]

My friend Leeana Tankersley, author of *Found Art: Discovering Beauty in Foreign Places,* blogged this beautiful tribute to her Navy Seal husband on Memorial Day. This is what positive reinforcement can sound like:

> Today, I want to say something to my husband, my silent war-rior, who so amazingly coexists at the tip of the spear and the heart of our home:
>
> Dear Steve,
>
> Sometimes I forget that you are part of this elite brotherhood of SEALs. I see you changing diapers and making dinner and

putting gas in my car and throwing the kids in the air in the front yard.

And then—all of a sudden, out of nowhere—I'm reminded of how much you do that I never see and never know. I'm reminded of how hard you've been pushed and how much is demanded of you. I am aware that you are remarkable.

Thank you for choosing to do the difficult work of being a faithful father and husband while you, simultaneously, do the difficult work of freedom fighting. I will never know what this demands of you.

Thank you for going to work every day and for coming home, too—neither of which is easy.

Thank you for being all in, all the time.

Thank you for chasing adventure and for taking me along for the ride.

Thank you for loving me.

Today, I want you to know I believe in you. I believe in us. And I am so incredibly proud of you.

Fair winds and following seas, my Pirate,
Leeana[6]

Like Leeana, may we choose to notice the faithful father and warrior at our side.

Notice Today:

What are three things your husband does well as a father?

1.

2.

3.

Nurture Today:

Allow your husband to parent the kids using his unique style. Don't try to make him into a clone of you. Tell him today—or write a note—expressing your appreciation. If you have belittled him as a father in the past, apologize and tell him you're going to trust him more in the future.

Take a Number

"Your desire will be for your husband."
GENESIS 3:16

I f I tell you about this outing, you may think we don't get out enough. For a big night on the town, my family likes to go to the Spanish supermarket. My kids are learning Spanish, so we think it's highly educational, plus the free hot tortillas are delicious. One day, we walked up to the meat counter and giggled about the pigs' feet and intestines. We'd pass on those, but we were going to get some marinated chicken. Looking up, we saw the big electronic number that showed who was being served. We looked for the machine and found it. It read, "Take a number."

I wonder if your husband ever feels that way.

Forget having sex. The kids are up with runny noses.

Take a number.

Can we reschedule our breakfast date? Mary called me for coffee, and you know she's going through such a hard time.

Take a number.

The women's ministry team needs me to create centerpieces for the luncheon, so I just don't have time.

Take a number.

Goodbye Big Man on Campus. Hello Low Man on the Totem Pole.

The Baby Universe

It's a rhyme that has described a happy family for years: First comes love, then comes marriage, then comes baby in the baby carriage. Each step gets progressively more challenging, especially the passage into parenthood, which often leaves the husband scratching his head and wondering, *What happened to my wife?*

My friends Matt and Joanie research everything. Before tying the knot, they immersed themselves in premarital books and discussions. Matt said he felt incredibly prepared to become a husband, but when it came to being a father, he was blindsided.

> Nobody prepared me for what would happen to a woman and her body after having babies. Forget about having sex when you both fall into bed at 10:00 p.m. utterly exhausted. We had to relearn how to be a couple again. No one warned us how difficult that can be after children. [7]

Derek, a father with a one-year-old and new baby, was honest enough to say, "Internally I felt jealous of my new baby. I think most fathers feel this way. Now my wife and I don't have time to talk. We have to make time for important discussions or else they don't happen." [8]

My family was listening to a Sesame Street CD, and one of the silly songs was about an "everything in the wrong place" ball. I wanted to liven up an otherwise normal weeknight, so I told everyone, including James, to dress up with everything in the wrong place for dinner. Ethan came out with a pair of (clean) underwear on his head. Noelle had all her clothes on backward. I had two different earrings, my glasses on upside down, and a bathing suit on my head. But James took the cake wearing diapers stuck together all across his bottom and more diapers making a diagonal sash across his chest like Rambo Dad. Ready to save the world, one diaper at a time. I had to laugh as I wondered, *Is this what a grown man must do to get some attention around here?*

In the book *On Becoming Babywise*, Gary Ezzo and Robert Bucknam write:

> Too often when a child enters a family, parents leave their first love: each other. The spotlight shifts to illuminate the children, and the marriage gets lost in space. Typically—and ironically—this occurs in the name of good parenting...Rather than welcoming children to the family, children are treated as the center of the family universe. [9]

National youth speaker and author Mark Matlock adds:

It's really easy to let your kids become the centerpiece of your family's life. One of the things that make a home healthy and happy is when Mom and Dad are inviting their kids into their relationship. Their relationship is the anchor piece instead of the children being what it's all about. We'll tell our kids, "Go inside. Mom and Dad are on the deck talking." We try to protect our time.[10]

Don't Forget the Giant

There's a giant person living in your house who needs your attention: your husband. He's the one who can blend in with the furniture if you're not careful. You're used to him being around. You figure he's a capable human being who can meet his own needs. Think again.

One night James asked if I could get the kids to bed quickly because he wanted to give me a massage. You would think I would jump at the chance, but after kissing the kids goodnight, I went to the kitchen. I washed baby bottles, put dishes in the dishwasher, and packed up the diaper bag with what I needed for church the next day.

All this clanging around in the kitchen was ticking James off—and rightfully so. Hadn't he communicated he wanted me to bed early for my massage? When I walked into the room, he looked tired.

"If you don't want to give me a massage, that's fine," I mumbled lamely. "I took a long time in the kitchen."

He asked why I couldn't just leave the dishes in the sink. In the morning, he would have done them happily.

I had made the wrong choice.

Many times we wives run around doing all these things we think are urgent, but we leave the important things undone. Things like respecting our spouse's requests. Good grief, I didn't respond to a request to give me a massage!

52 Dates

Bob and Jana have four children ranging from elementary school to college age. As a business owner, Bob works long hours and also umpires a few evenings out of the week. Jana busies herself with working as a teacher, caring for the kids, managing the house, serving on the board of her church…you know the drill. Bit by bit, Bob was feeling neglected, as if he were Jana's last priority. The kids seemed to get more attention than he did. This feeling of being last on the list ate away at Bob, but like many men, he was too macho to say anything.

Men are in a dilemma. If they say they need something, they risk coming across as nerds who can't do anything or needy boys who want their mommies. Bob didn't want to look weak and he didn't want to dump one more thing on his wife's already full plate. *"I see you're busy, honey, can you take care of me too?"* So he silently struggled with his feeling of abandonment.

Finally he realized he had a choice. He could sit there feeling neglected or he could tell his wife, who was his best friend, he was hurting. Thankfully he chose the latter, and of course Jana responded immediately. She figured everything was fine between them since Bob hadn't given any signs of being frustrated. They decided to have a weekly date night to make sure they would stay connected. Once they had a regular date night in place, Bob's feeling of being neglected disappeared.

For Christmas, Jana made Bob a very special box. Inside the box were fifty-two slips of paper, each containing the description of a different date she had made up. (Jana and Bob were kind enough to share twenty-five of these date ideas on page 155.) A few days before each weekend, they pull out a slip of paper to see what their date night will be. A walk on the beach. Cheese and crackers at home looking at old family photo albums. Hiking a nearby trail. They not only enjoy the date itself but all the anticipation that goes along with it. Because of that creative date box, Bob knows his wife cares about connecting with him every day. He no longer feels he's at the bottom of the list. Just like the kids in the nursery, he's got a standing date with his wife.

Dave Carder, author of *Close Calls,* says:

> Remember when you were dating? If you had an hour and half for lunch, and you had to drive one hour round-trip just to spend thirty minutes with your boyfriend, you would still go. Too many married couples rely on the mornings and the evenings as the only time they will see their spouse. Those are the two worst times of the day. You need to see your spouse at odd and unusual times, and predictable times. And you would make that choice

if you had a girlfriend or boyfriend. You would accommodate them. And we don't do that in marriage. I know wives who won't go on expense-paid business trips with their husbands because it's too much trouble with the kids. That is foolish. Taking time off with your husband is the kind of thing you have to do if you want to make your marriage work.[11]

When was the last time you had a rendezvous with your husband, even when it was inconvenient? Make sure he knows he's number one on your list. Let him know he doesn't need a number to spend time with you.

Notice Today:

When you and your husband were dating, how often would you meet throughout the week? How did you flex and adjust your schedules to see each other?

Nurture Today:

Schedule to meet each other at an odd time. Have lunch or breakfast out together. Take a late-night walk. Do something out of the ordinary together.

Day 4

Money Talks

"Our money is all gone."
GENESIS 47:15

"My problem lies in reconciling my gross habits with my net income."—Errol Flynn
"Women prefer men who have something tender about them—especially the legal kind."—Kay Ingram
"Whoever said money can't buy happiness simply didn't know where to go shopping."—Bo Derek
"When I open my wallet, it squeaks."—James Pellicane

Do any of these quotes describe your attitude about money? My family has a saying, "If it's free, it's me." James and I are frugal, but we'll spend money on a quality experience (memory-making vacation) or a quality product (something you'll have for life). For many years, I've thought of compiling a top-ten list of our frugality, so here goes.

Top-Ten Ways You Know You're Frugal

1. After a fast-food meal, you raid the table for unused straws, ketchup pouches, plastic utensils, and napkins.

2. Your son tattles on his sister for leaving the bathroom light on more than five seconds after brushing her teeth.

3. You buy cologne at the dollar store.

4. You shop at thrift stores only when they have an additional 20 percent off.

5. You put down a shirt at a garage sale because they want two dollars for it.

6. The only new books your kids have are from the library.

7. You fill up on bread at the fancy restaurants because you can always box up the meal.

8. You never order anything but water to drink.

9. You bring a to-go bag for your Costco samples.

10. You tear your Kleenex in half before using it.

Savers and Spenders

While I was in New York City promoting my book *31 Days to a Younger You*, I met "The Money Couple," Scott and Bethany Palmer. In their book *First Comes Love, Then Comes Money*, they describe five money personalities: the saver, the spender, the risk taker, the security seeker, and the flyer. I suppose you can guess my primary money personality is saver, and so is my husband's.

Bethany and Scott are both primarily spenders, but their secondary money personality clashes. She's a risk taker. He's a security seeker. Bethany wanted to buy a piece of land. Scott went along with it even though he felt like he was going to throw up. It turned out to be a home run. Another time she found a donut franchise in Europe. He shut that down after researching the puffy pastries, and she agreed. Scott says, "Part of having clear and precise financial communication is once you trust each other, you can make those decisions. One can say, 'Let's do this.' The other can say, 'Great, let's talk about it.' It doesn't become a fight. It's an opportunity to learn more about each other."[12]

What if you don't have "clear and precise financial communication"? That's Marriage PhD level stuff. What if you're still in the sandbox fighting over toys with your husband? Scott suggests you start by eliminating financial surprises.

> Surprises hurt, surprises anger. Surprises give you a feeling of mistrust. Surprises are terrible. The way to take away money surprises is by understanding your spouse's money personality. My wife, my beloved, is a spender. So if she goes and spends money,

I'm anything but surprised. Oh, Beth went shopping. I wonder
what the damage is?[13]

James and I are both savers. Bethany and Scott are both spenders. That
makes the financial conversations a little bit easier because we can relate
to one another. But life can still work when two different money personalities come to the table, acknowledging that saving or spending is part of
their DNA and going from there.

> I don't wake up and look at Bethany and say, "I can't believe
> you have red hair." It's who she is. And the same is true with
> our money personalities. Does that mean that a spender can go
> out and charge a thousand dollars on new stereo equipment or
> designer handbags because it's their money personality? No, but
> now you have a frame of reference to understand each other's ten-
> dencies without resorting to name-calling.[14]

Scott remembers talking to a man who was upset because his wife
(a spender) wanted to plan a vacation they simply couldn't afford. She
called him cheap, and he was hurt. Scott understood that what the man
was really saying was, "I'm mad at my wife because she's disrespecting me."
Scott told the man, "You're not cheap. You're a saver. Your wife needs to
stop calling you cheap and to understand what your money personality
is." Instantly, the man's demeanor changed as he was understood and val-
idated instead of put down and mocked.

> It's an easy conversation to start. It's not about accusing, "You're
> a saver. You're a spender." It's about who are you and who am
> I? We pull couples up on the stage every time we speak and
> help them discover their money personalities. We had a couple
> that had been married thirty-eight years who just learned their
> money personality on stage. They were looking at each other
> like, "I haven't understood that about you for the last thirty-
> eight years."[15]

You don't want to go thirty-eight years before understanding the way
your husband is wired financially. Is he a saver, spender, risk taker, or security seeker? What are you? If you don't know, it's time to have a money talk
with your man this week.

Norman Vincent Peale said, "Empty pockets never held anyone back. Only empty heads and empty hearts can do that."[16]

Notice Today:

What money personality do you think your husband is? What are you?

Saver

Spender

Risk Taker

Security Seeker

Flyer (not too concerned about money, flying by the seat of their pants financially)

Nurture Today:

Recognize your husband's money personality as valid, and then schedule a money talk. Discuss what you can both do better to work as a team financially instead of working against each other. Decide together on one specific step to implement this month to get financially stronger.

Day 5

Working Blues

"How long, LORD, must I call for help, but you do not listen?"
HABAKKUK 1:2

Can you imagine losing your job eleven times in twelve months? That's the financial nightmare Sam and Maria lived through in the 1990s. Sam was laid off ten times when ten tire stores closed their doors during a time of recession and uncertainty. When he lost yet another job, he bore the weight of the world on his shoulders. Add that to a long list of problems: a repossessed Bronco, an old Plymouth that died, a bicycle found in a dumpster and stolen a week later, an overdrawn bank account, and an eviction notice and deadline for $1,300 in back rent. Did I mention they had a new baby girl?

As a new Christian, Maria prayed fervently, "How long, LORD, must I call for help, but you do not listen?" (Habakkuk 1:2). She didn't understand how, but childlike faith took over and Maria dramatically changed her attitude. "I stopped acting like a damsel in distress and became, instead, the builder and keeper of a fortress for our family. I became an oasis for my husband's weary mind and body so God could renew his strength before another day of battle."

Maria proposed a crazy plan. They would pawn his shotgun, rifle, and her wedding ring to start a husband-and-wife cleaning business. They walked out of the pawnshop with $180, which they used for groceries, diapers, gas, bright-yellow fliers for their new business, matching shorts and T-shirts, old towels at the thrift store, brooms, buckets, and squeegees. They needed $1,300 in seven days or they would be evicted.

As God would have it, an old acquaintance asked what they were up to. Turns out she managed a building that needed the inside windows of twelve floors cleaned. Would they be willing to do it for $1,300? Maria remembers,

> For six consecutive nights, Sam and I cleaned windows and glass office partitions from 6:00 p.m. until 3:00 a.m., talking about God's goodness until we were too tired to scrub, squeegee, and talk at the same time. I had never felt so tired and refreshed at the same time, and this was just the beginning of the journey.[17]

Keeper of the Fortress

Maria made an important decision early in her marriage. No longer a damsel in distress, she turned into a window-washing mom entrepreneur. She decided not to guilt, berate, despise, or shame her husband for his string of layoffs. Instead, look at the words she used to describe her role as a wife: *The builder and keeper of the fortress. An oasis.* If your husband is unemployed, overemployed, or going through rough times financially, those are some excellent titles for what you can do to bless your man.

I heard Marjorie Blanchard say that at the Ken Blanchard Companies' U.S. headquarters, the receptionist sign reads "Director of First Impressions." Not much turnover at that desk since the job has been defined and championed. As a wife, you have a sign too. Especially when your husband is going through unemployment, your sign reads "Keeper of the Fortress" and "Oasis." That kind of love will balance out the rejection he is constantly facing in the marketplace and among his peers.

When my son was four, he got his toy cars taken away from him because he had been disobedient. He was crying his heart out, and his two-year-old sister, Noelle, walked over to him and handed him her favorite toy car. "Here you go, Ethan," she said. Ethan looked up, took the toy, and stopped crying. "She cheered me up," he said very quietly to me. A few days later, he mentioned Noelle's kindness again. "Remember when Noelle cheered me up by giving me her car?" That small act had made quite an impression.

Some days our husbands get their cars taken away, and we find them having a full-blown pity party. They don't need a lecture or judgment from us. What they need is an act of kindness. That's the kind of warmth that will be remembered for quite some time.

Stripped of Identity

It's been two years since another friend, John, lost his job as an architectural sales representative. He loved his job working on commercial buildings. John said,

> Here we were on track to a great career and things were going as we had planned. The first three months of being unemployed was this overwhelming numbing sensation. I can't believe what just happened. Then it was talking myself through it. This must be God's will. There must be something on the other side of the hill. The longer unemployment continues, the more it's going to magnify itself. When my job was taken away, it really stripped away my identity. It's certainly my responsibility to try to manage that emotion, but sometimes it gets the best of you. It's helpful when wives have good awareness of what's going on and keep in mind that it's temporary. It's not a permanent state your husband is going to be in. Don't question him, give him the third degree, or try to fix him.[18]

It's easy for the husband or wife to feel pessimistic when job hunting. Interviews come and opportunities go. Hope rises only to be squelched by a potential employer's rejection or lack of response. The unconditional love and respect of a wife can truly carry a husband along during the dark days of unemployment. Conversely, a wife's disapproval and unkindness can drive the nails in the coffin.

Picture an old-fashioned filmstrip. It's long and skinny, each square a different photograph. We tend to focus on just one image—such as the unemployment image—and picture that's all there is in life. But we forget that one image is only part of a much greater compilation of images that make up the filmstrip of our lives.

If your husband has to walk through a season of unemployment, he wants to know he's not alone. You will walk beside him, sometimes giving a word of encouragement, sometimes biting your tongue, and sometimes telling him to get back on the horse.

When tough times come, meditate on 2 Corinthians 4:8-9: "We are hard pressed on every side, but not crushed; perplexed, but not in despair; persecuted, but not abandoned; struck down, but not destroyed."

Notice Today:

If your husband is having a rough time at work, consider how discouraged he must feel on some days. Take a moment to put yourself in his shoes.

Nurture Today:

Make your man feel like a man again by…pursuing him sexually this week, cooking his favorite meal, going to a sports game, or giving him a massage.

Guide 2

Domestic Tranquillity

Respect
*Your husband needs to be
honored in his own home.*

Eros

Attraction

Mutual Activities

Day 6

Alpha Dog

*Wives, submit yourselves to your own
husbands as you do to the Lord.*

Ephesians 5:22

Since I've never been a dog owner, I don't have many conversations about dogs. But I do remember one talk from years ago about dogs and leadership. My friends Ken and Brittney were explaining how dogs are pack animals by nature. Every pack has a leader known as the alpha dog. This alpha dog makes decisions and calls the shots. Ken described how his dog would try to assert himself as alpha by jumping up to sit on the very top of the couch. Putting himself physically higher than Ken made the dog the leader. Understanding this, Ken trained the dog to stay off the top of the couch and sit below on the floor, establishing Ken as the master instead. Once his dog understood Ken was the alpha dog in the home, it was a walk in the park. Dogs respect an alpha when they see it.

Did you know there's an alpha dog in your house (and it's not you)?

The S Word

No, this *S* word is not *sex*; it's *submission*. Although the seemingly archaic idea of submitting to a man has many Christian women up in arms, the biblical command to wives has not changed through the centuries. The New Testament writers make it clear in three passages:

- "Wives, submit yourselves to your own husbands as you do to the Lord" (Ephesians 5:22).

- "Wives, submit yourselves to your husbands, as is fitting in the Lord" (Colossians 3:18).

- "Wives, in the same way submit yourselves to your own husbands so that, if any of them do not believe the word, they may be won over without words by the behavior of their wives" (1 Peter 3:1).

In all three instances, the wife is addressed first and then the husband. Doesn't it make sense that when you take the first step to submit to your husband, your husband will find it much easier to fulfill his responsibility of loving you as Christ loved the church? Don't require your husband to act loving before you submit to him. You submit first out of obedience to God and allow God to do the work in the heart of your man.

Matthew Henry's commentary says it this way: "The love which God requires from the husband in behalf of his wife will make amends for the subjection which he demands from her to her husband; and the prescribed subjection of the wife will be an abundant return for the love of the husband which God has made her due."[1]

In other words, God will make it worth your while. When you submit, your husband will be rewarded for his love toward you. On the flip side, your submission will be a small price to pay for the lavish love of your husband.

But what if your husband's love is anything but lavish? He may be lazy, harsh, insensitive, or foolish. Are *you* really supposed to submit to *him*? The answer is still a resounding yes. In his series "A Biblical Portrait of Marriage," Bruce Wilkinson says, "Why would a woman who is equal to a man in the image of God ever give away her life to a man? For two reasons: Because she realizes that's exactly why she was created. And number two, she will be the happiest and most fulfilled in the role God has made."[2]

In Genesis 2:18, we read that it was not good for man to be alone, so God made a helper suitable for him. The woman was created for the man and not vice versa. Our role is that of helper. My childhood pastor, Glen Cole, has been in ministry more than fifty-five years, and he gives these helpful insights about submission in marriage:

> It's the real foundation of God's creation for both man and wife. It doesn't imply dominance. It implies a togetherness that puts

the other's interests above their own. Without that kind of under-standing, there are huge problems and difficulties. Anything with two heads is a monstrosity and belongs in a traveling circus. In marriage, it really is true. You cannot have two heads. Someone has to have the final word, particularly if the couple is locked in a disagreement. The female has to give in to the divine order that God created to bring about the right direction for the family. There has to be someone who is responsible for the final decision.[3]

You've probably heard the saying, "He may be the head, but I'm the neck." God has given us a tremendous position of influence in our homes. Wives don't have to be robots that simply chant "Yes, master" and "Right away, dear." We can respectfully express our opinions, but then we must peacefully walk away, allowing the husband to lead as God intended. Bob Lepine says,

> Mary Ann laughs that she wants me to lead as long as I do exactly what she wants me to do. What she's really saying is, "I want to lead. I want you to be the one out front doing it, but I want to control things behind the scenes." I think that's an issue for a lot of women. They think they must be in control of their environ-ment and circumstances in order to be safe. That's an illusion in the first place. You're never in control of your environment or cir-cumstances. Even if you were in control, that doesn't mean that the decisions you make would be the right one or the safest one.[4]

The Bible reveals the principle that wives are to submit to their hus-bands *as to the Lord*. Trust God that He will make it up to you if your hus-band is unloving. Second Samuel 22:21 says, "The LORD has dealt with me according to *my* righteousness; according to the cleanness of *my* hands he has rewarded me." When you stand before God someday, He's not going to ask about what your husband did. He's going to ask what you did.

Everyday Alpha

What does submission look like in everyday life? Hop into my mini-van for two day-to-day examples.

Tacos El Gordo. We were headed to a Mexican taco paradise to celebrate my mom's birthday. We were supposed to leave at 4:00, but we didn't get motoring until 4:30. To make things worse, the gas light went on. James grabbed the car manual, and I assumed he was trying to check how many miles we could drive with the gas light on. I started to say, "Dear, I really don't think we should get on the freeway with the gas light—" But he stopped me from talking. Submission stops talking. But what do we do so many times, ladies? We keep talking. James flipped through the manual, not to check about the gas gauge but to take cash out of it for the gas station. He knew what he was doing all along. I just needed to keep my mouth shut and let him take care of the problem.

To the Nursery. We were visiting a church, and on the way there, I told James I would take our baby Lucy to the nursery.

"Nope, I'll take her," he said.

"Honey, you've been looking forward to visiting this church and hearing the pastor, so I will—"

He interrupted and said again with more firmness, "Nope, the decision is made. I will take Lucy to the nursery."

This didn't make any sense to me, but since James was so definitive and now getting irritated, I realized I'd better let it go. James made that decision because Lucy is clingier with me. When he dropped her off in the unfamiliar nursery, she didn't even shed a tear.

Your husband was created by God to be the leader of your home, the captain of the minivan, and the head coach of the team. Are you trusting your alpha dog to lead your pack today?

Notice Today:

Do you treat your husband as the leader in your home? If not, what is preventing you? If yes, what is your motivation for letting him lead?

Nurture Today:

The next time your husband suggests something you disagree with, bite your tongue and go with the flow. As long as it's morally acceptable, you can show some flexibility.

Day 7

Big Hunk

My beloved is like a gazelle or a young stag.
SONG OF SONGS 2:9

When you married your husband, wasn't he the Big Hunk in your life? Remember, you used to practically salivate when he entered the room. Your heart pitter-pattered, you felt dizzy and giddy, and your palms were sweaty. That sweet and scrumptious man was divinity.

Fast-forward the tape five years. Ten years. Twenty. Now your Big Hunk is more like a Big Lug or a Big Bonehead or even a Big Pain in the Rear End. What happened? When did you make the switch from Big Hunk (you gorgeous man) to Snickers (wait until I tell my girlfriends about this one)?

The things about your spouse that attracted you at first are now driving you crazy. When you were dating, you loved your husband's quiet side. You talked to your heart's content to a captive (and captivated) audience. Now you're ticked because your husband doesn't talk. Before saying "I do," his strength made you feel completely safe and taken care of. Now you think he's an overbearing dictator.

Marriage has a way of putting a magnifying glass over what's wrong instead of what's right. If we were completely honest, even if our husbands did one hundred things right and one thing wrong, what would we fixate on? That one wrong thing. Bring on the Snickers.

Lucky Me

My James would astonish you. He makes our family breakfast most mornings. He does diapers and takes care of the kids when they're sick at night. He provides for our family cheerfully and diligently. He washes dishes and even cleans the grout on the kitchen island. He practices the piano with our kids. He doesn't watch sports on TV and sometimes gives me a massage at the end of the day. He's godly and relational, perfectly talkative, and even likes some chick flicks.

I know, I know. How did I get this lucky? But believe me, just like any other two human beings living together, we have our rough spots. James has high standards, and it seems normal to him that I should too. That sounds extremely reasonable until you play it out with a flesh-and-blood imperfect wife.

The other day our twenty-month-old Lucy was chewing on a piece of paper. I know that's not good, but she's our third child, and to be honest, I needed to write a chapter in this very book you're holding. A little extra fiber didn't seem to be such a bad idea. Lucy was enjoying that piece of paper so much. It would buy me a few solid minutes.

James walked in and said in disgust, "Sweetheart." In that one word, he communicated volumes. The translation: "What are you, stupid or something? Do you not see that our baby is eating a piece of paper? Come on— you know better than that!" I felt instantly humiliated and hurt. I went into passive-aggressive mode and sarcastic thoughts churned in my mind. *I guess I'm not perfect like you are.*

I began to tear my husband down in my mind. *He's so demanding. He's such a know-it-all.* My admiring Big Hunk attitude was quickly turning into a bunch of little Snickers. I breathed a quick prayer, and the Holy Spirit helped me calmly say to James, "This is not a big thing, but it would really help me if you corrected me in a more pleasant way. We're not all as perfect as you." This made us both laugh, mostly because it's true. The trouble with having a confident, wise husband is he can grow frustrated with the incompetence surrounding him. And sometimes that incompetence is me.

A few days later, James came home with a dozen roses. He said, "Sometimes I don't treat you like a lady, and I want to get better at that. Will you help me do that?" Big Hunk, welcome back.

The Hunk You've Got

Before you can have a happy husband, you've got to be happy with the hunk you've got. I remember when I signed my first book contract.

What a reason to celebrate. In Pellicane fashion, we didn't go out to a restaurant for overpriced desserts. We were going to splurge and buy two gallons of ice cream at our local grocery store for a whopping five dollars on sale. James went to buy the ice cream, and all I asked was that one of the flavors be chocolate. I was dreaming of moose tracks or double chocolate chip. Guess what James came home with to celebrate *my* book contract? Cookies and cream for the kids and caramel pecan crunch for us. To say I was disappointed would be an understatement. Oh, and did I mention I was pregnant at the time?

Was it really too hard to get some kind of chocolate ice cream as a splurge for the celebrating pregnant author? What was my husband thinking when he picked out those flavors?

I took one bite of the caramel pecan crunch and put my spoon down. "It's too sweet," I said coldly. I was going to pout out this dessert because Mr. Perfect messed up the painfully simple order.

My son Ethan was four at the time, and he noticed my long face and angry eyes. "Mom," he said, "you should be content with what you have."

Ouch. Ethan was right. Sometimes you get caramel when you crave chocolate. Sometimes your husband does things that aren't very "hunk-like." But then again, I'm sure there are many days when I'm not exactly a princess (unless you count Sleeping Beauty when she's still asleep). Do yourself and your husband a favor. Be thankful for the hunk you've got.

Public Raves

It's especially denigrating when a wife puts down her husband in front of other men. I cringe when a wife says something like, "We would like to go, but with my husband's salary, we just can't afford it." Imagine how that makes him feel. Or there's the prayer request in Sunday school, "Pray for my husband. He can't find a job." The demoralized husband wants to fade into the woodwork. David Frisbie says about his wife, Lisa,

> If Lisa is talking to her mother or her girlfriends or her daughters or people at work, no matter where she is, no matter what she's doing, I don't have to watch my back. Because I know if she talks about me, she will be positive and encouraging. That is priceless. What that does in a marriage is absolutely beyond value.

We do see women in the church who are unconsciously running down their husbands all the time. And the result is other people pick up some of that and begin to think of their husbands in that way. Within the family it's just poison.[5]

Snickers about your husband poison a marriage. But praising your Big Hunk yields big results. Make the decision today to be like the wife in Proverbs 31. Let this statement from Proverbs 31:12 describe your life: "I bring my husband good, not harm, all the days of my life."

Notice Today:

Make a list of five things you find attractive about your Big Hunk:

1.

2.

3.

4.

5.

Nurture Today:

Have you spoken poorly about your husband to your family or friends? Listen to the way you talk about your husband in the next week. Choose your words wisely and repent when you don't.

Day 8

Don't Go Changing

How good and pleasant it is
when God's people live together in unity!
PSALM 133:1

I read about a young husband who forgot he was married. The day after his honeymoon, he returned to work like normal. Absentmindedly, he drove home to his mother's suburban house instead of to his bride. You can only imagine the welcome he received when he arrived at his new home three hours late. The honeymoon phase quickly ended and his dinner went up in flames. His wife literally burned the dinner. Wouldn't you?

You must make many changes after you get married—realizing you have a new address being one of them. But unfortunately, some wives don't stop with just the new address. They decide they want to change their man.

When Tshaka Armstrong was first married at age twenty, his wife, Kelli, was in for a surprise. "She married a boy who was trying to figure out how to be a husband and a dad on the job," Tshaka said. "I was a mama's boy. My wife and I got separated mainly because of my family intruding on the relationship, which I wasn't standing up to."[6] But God intervened and after five years of separation, Tshaka and Kelli reconciled.

Marital counseling gave them tools to understand their differences. Kelli was raised by a single parent. She was used to getting things done on her own. Tshaka was an easygoing, passive-aggressive, recovering people pleaser. She's a five-foot pit bull; he's a six-foot, 240-pound teddy bear. She uses a PC computer; he uses a Mac. By their own admission, they don't get along on anything.

But when Tshaka stepped up as the leader and Kelli, despite her discomfort, allowed him to be the man, things started to change. He said, "Wives have to give husbands space to be who they are. That's a fundamental relationship characteristic. Love each other enough to allow each other to be who we are. Now we have the marriage we should have had in the beginning."[7]

Vive La Difference

I love the story my mentor, international speaker, and author Pam Farrel tells about her husband, Bill, and his love for coffee. Bill jokes that Pam, who doesn't drink coffee, is naturally caffeinated by God, and it takes him three cups just to catch up with her. The downside of Bill's need for java is his habit of leaving coffee cups in the garage, in the car, in the closet, on the patio, in the office, in the bathroom—anywhere but the dishwasher. Instead of setting a course to change her dish-impaired husband, here's how Pam handled those pesky mugs:

> Coffee is a part of what makes Bill, well, Bill. One day, as we were preparing to move and I was doing that last load of dishes, I realized it was composed of all coffee mugs. Forty-seven of them to be exact. It made me smile because years ago, I decided to pray for Bill every time I saw one of his empty, displaced mugs. I was seeking to apply the principle, "love covers over a multitude of sins" (1 Peter 4:8). I learned to embrace the ever-reappearing dirty coffee mug with fond affection because it reminds me of my hardworkin' man who requires caffeine to do all the wonderful acts of service that benefit so many—including me. Praying for Bill when I see a coffee mug, even when I travel and might be away from him, has become my life rhythm.[8]

High Above the Arboretum

My James is a free spirit, and I am a rules keeper. If I see a sign that says, "No Trespassing," I don't trespass. With James it's another story. In our first few months of marriage, we visited the lovely Dallas Arboretum. We paid our admission and began our tour of the sixty-six-acre gardens. After we had been walking for some time, James looked through the wrought-iron fence and said, "Look, I can see our car." Indeed the parking lot was on the other side of the fence. We were tired of walking. To return to our car would mean walking all the way back to the entrance just to walk that same length back to the parking lot. (You know what's coming next, right?)

"Let's jump the fence," James said.

Okay, there are many problems running through my mind. One, the fence is eight feet tall and I have never climbed a fence in my life. Two, what would this look like? How would the other people know we were climbing *out* of the arboretum instead of *into* it?

"Nope," I announced. "I can't do it."

Before you could say "Happy Husband," James locked his hands together and prepared to hoist me over the fence. "We are not walking all the way through this park to get to our car. Just climb the fence," he said firmly.

After protesting and stalling, I finally put my foot in his hands and grabbed the fence. I swung one leg over and then froze. I was terrified. I'd never sat on an eight-foot, wrought-iron fence before, plus I was crazy nervous about doing something I felt was wrong. People were beginning to come into view, and I was mortified beyond measure. To make matters worse, I started to cry and kept thinking, *I can't believe James made me get up here.*

"Just throw your leg over and jump," James said, growing increasingly frustrated.

He thought I was stuck on stupid. I thought he was the most unfeeling, unkind groom ever. What knight would perch his princess on a fence of death?

I finally got the nerve to throw my leg over the other side. I tumbled down into the parking lot in a heap of tears and embarrassment.

There was nothing fond about that moment then, but I sure do love that story now. Without my free-spirited husband, where would I get my crazy stories? I've tamed him a bit through the years (which sometimes I actually regret), so I'm trying to be less rigid and go with the flow. After all, life high above the arboretum is quite memorable.

Moo Time

My brother-in-law John and his wife, Christine, have been married for two years. Like most couples, they have discovered there are many things in life they don't agree on, including dessert. Out to dinner one night, they were given three dessert options. The only one that sounded appealing to her was the chocolate crème brûlée.

"That's the one thing I do not want," John said.

"And I don't eat either of the other two," Christine said.

Deadlocked over dessert, they headed for Maggie Moo's ice-cream parlor. They each got their own cone with custom toppings mixed in. They sat down and *finally* enjoyed their agreeable desserts.

Differences are inevitable. Don't set out to change your husband. Instead, learn how to enjoy your differences by understanding one another better. Separate cones for ice cream may be a good start.

Notice Today:

What's a difference between you and your husband that drives you nuts? What difference do you think drives him nuts?

Nurture Today:

Thinking of your husband's difference, write down how that difference may add depth and strength to your marriage. For instance, my husband being a free spirit has led us to opportunities that I would have never tried were it up to me.

Day 9

20,000 Words

Anxiety weighs down the heart,
but a kind word cheers it up.

PROVERBS 12:25

Can you relate to any of the following wives?

- *The Complaining Wife*—"Janet's husband takes her to fancy restaurants. This place is such a dump."

- *The Nagging Wife*—"When are you going to get around to taking me out to dinner? You've been talking about it for weeks and I'm still waiting."

- *The Angry Wife*—"Why do we always eat where you want to eat? Our whole life revolves around your selfishness."

- *The Ice Princess Wife*—Silence (you might as well be eating alone).

Would you want to talk to any of these people? Me neither. Yet how many times do we act like this when our husbands don't do what we want?

For many wives, there's a disconnect between espousing to be a good Christian wife while verbally shredding our husbands to pieces. You might not even be aware of it. Maybe you are killing your mate with a fury of explosive words or slowly poisoning him with subtle put-downs. The trick is to make ugly words the exception in our lives and not the rule. Your words matter to your husband and to God.

Consider this poem about the power of words:

A careless word may kindle strife.
A cruel word may wreck a life,
A bitter word may hate instill;
A brutal word may smite and kill,
A gracious word may smooth the way;
A joyous word may light the day.
A timely word may lessen stress;
A loving word may heal and bless.
   —Author Unknown

Comedian Tim Hawkins has been married to Heather for eighteen years. He says about verbal affirmation,

> I think if women would realize when we have earned it, we do need positive reinforcement. Everything's not okay all the time. We do like to be honored in a quiet way. We don't need a big fanfare. Just find out how your man likes to be honored. Maybe it's a quick word off to the side, "You did a great job today." Little affirmations go a long way (and coming to bed naked, that would be great too).[9]

Treasure, Don't Trash

My friend Betsy has been married for forty-two years and shares these insights about bringing healing and blessing to our marriages: "The main one is to complement, not compete, and to treasure and not trash. The power of humility in a marriage can't be diminished. We are both headstrong and like to get our point across. It's better to have a relationship than be right all the time."[10]

Actor Kevin Sorbo (*Hercules, Soul Surfer*) agrees. The biggest thing he and his wife, Sam, have discussed is not to belittle each other and not to constantly correct each other. "You don't have to flex your intelligence all the time," he says. "If anything, it's being more supportive with each other and more of a teammate with each other than being the person who is always cutting down. That is something that will make a relationship go away in a hurry."[11]

If someone were to repeat all the things you say to your husband, would it be "news that's fit to print?" Are you heaping on praise, encouragement, and honor? Psychologist and author David Clarke says that verbal respect is the lifeblood of a man.

> Women have a need for this too, but this runs so deep in the man. Most women are frankly lousy at it. Women get into the habit of praising only when the job is done how they want it done, when it's done really great. Well, you know, you've got to learn to praise mediocre. Praise pretty good. Because the guy will stop doing the job if he's not praised. He'll think, *It didn't mean much to her* or *I can't please her*. In time, you can gently add your suggestions, but at the beginning, you just want to say thank you.[12]

Treasure your husband's efforts to please you and provide for your family. Don't trash what he does either to his face or behind his back. Your words matter more to him than anyone else's. Pastor and best-selling author David Jeremiah says it this way about his wife, Donna:

> Because I live sort of a public life, lots of people say nice things to me. And I'm always grateful for that. But if I could take everything everybody says to me and put it all up in one place, it doesn't measure even half of the worth and value of what Donna says to me. Her words weigh more than all the words of everyone else. That's not just me. That's everyone. You've got to be your husband's cheerleader. Be his number one fan. Let him know. Don't assume that he knows.[13]

Does your husband know from your words—not the words you spoke on your wedding day, but the words you speak to him today—that you respect him? Have you praised him lately on his character, his appearance, or his abilities?

Bruce Wilkinson encourages wives to ask smart questions: "The question that must be asked from a wife to a husband is, 'How can I help you? What would you like me to do? How can I help you reach your dream? What can I do to enable you to become the man you are here to be?'"[14]

Imagine the impact of those words when spoken sincerely to your spouse. It's been said that a woman speaks on average twenty thousand words per day. Let's make the above-average decision to use some of those twenty thousand words to tell our husbands how much we respect and admire them.

Notice Today:

Write something you really appreciate about your husband. It could be something about his character or something he has done for you lately, like put gas in the car or fix a computer problem.

Nurture Today:

Tell him out loud or in a note what you wrote above. Be sure to be very specific about what he did and how it made you proud of him.

Day 10

Brew It

Be kind and compassionate to one another,
forgiving each other, just as in Christ God forgave you.

EPHESIANS 4:32

James usually makes the oatmeal at our house. He sets the timer for six minutes and walks away until the timer beeps. One morning I was feeling especially productive. I started the oatmeal and set the timer for six minutes. I went into the bathroom and started to shower, expecting that when James heard the timer, he would take care of the oatmeal. After all, he was within earshot of the timer when I left it. When it boiled over six-and-a-half minutes later, whose fault was it? Shouldn't James have heard the timer and put that all together?

I never *told* James to take care of the oatmeal. He had left the kitchen long ago. That whole sticky oatmeal mess was my fault. I had undercommunicated to my husband and overcooked our breakfast.

I wonder how many times we undercommunicate to our husbands just to overcook emotionally? In my oatmeal scenario, all I had to say was, "Honey, when the timer beeps, could you turn off the stove?" One sentence would have kept the situation from boiling over.

Please Understand Me

Curt and Elizabeth Hendley lived in a perfect storm of stress and tension. Curt had been unemployed for over a year, so they were living with his mom who was undergoing treatment for breast cancer. They had a new baby and a one-year-old. Curt said,

> I had a great deal of insecurity about being a husband and a father,
> just due to my background of my parents divorcing when I was
> ten. Being out of work for so long and having two small kids and
> having to live with my mother in my early thirties was humili-
> ating. I felt like I was not being a good husband or father. Not
> being a good man in general.[15]

Consumed by his own stress and insecurity, it never crossed Curt's mind that Elizabeth was hurting too. He figured, *What does she have to worry about? She stays home all day.* You already know the answer to that. She had a newborn and a one-year-old to care for, which is enough to make any sane woman lose it. Add to that living with your mother-in-law, who needed care after having a double mastectomy, and it was a terribly difficult time punctuated by regular misunderstandings and arguments.

When Curt finally explained to Elizabeth how and why he was stressed and feeling unfit as a husband and father, the light went on for her.

> One reason she didn't know what I was going through is I didn't
> tell her. Since my problem was different from hers, my problem
> wouldn't occur to her unless I said something. When I told her,
> it was a real revelation. We might have avoided fights a lot earlier
> if we would have understood each other's perspective earlier.[16]

P90X Buddies

After my third baby, James wanted to help me lose the baby weight. Can you see the fight coming? We became workout buddies, beginning ninety days of an intense home workout program called P90X. James wakes up earlier than I do. I hug the pillow, lying in the fetal position until the last possible second. About a month into the workout routine, James concluded my lagging in bed meant I was disinterested and wanted to quit. Nothing could have been further from the truth. I knew I needed some-one to kick me out of bed to lose those baby pounds.

We were at a birthday party when, to my shock, I overheard him say to a friend, "Do you want to do P90X with me?" He was ditching me—his wife—to work out with a friend, leaving me and my big-after-baby body behind. I was fuming.

After that party, I headed to a Mary Kay makeover party. Driving there, I was so mad. Why would my husband walk away from our exercise commitment to each other without even consulting me? I prayed in the car, *Lord, help me calm down. Forgive me for being so angry.* The time in the car helped me decompress. I tried to think of it from James's perspective. Maybe he was being overly friendly to his buddy because his friend was going through a hard time? I didn't know. My feelings of anger lessened, and when I got home, we talked about it right away.

He realized he'd made a big mistake and regretted it. He thought I didn't want to exercise together anymore and this would give me an out. James's part was apologizing. Mine was accepting his apology and forgetting about it. Not reminding him of his insensitive mistake every time we put in the workout DVD, but forgetting about it. Incidentally, James's friend never took up his offer, and we finished P90X how we started: side by side.

Before Punching Your Husband, Read This

Motivational speaker Zig Ziglar married his wife, Jeane, aka "the redhead" in 1946. He writes, "Many marriages would be better if the husband and the wife clearly understood that they are on the same side."[17]

When you disagree with your husband, remember whose side you're on. It's you and him against a mutual problem. That *problem* is the enemy, not your spouse. Take the target off your spouse's back. "In light of the world," says Tshaka Armstrong, "I see us as warriors fighting back-to-back. We can't be fighting everything outside our door back-to-back if we're face-to-face fighting each other."[18]

The next time you're tempted to knock your husband out, try the following four steps first.

Seek God. Pray before losing control. I find that a sincere quick prayer for wisdom does wonders. You may only have time to think, *Help, God.* Other times, you can pray longer about what's bugging you in the relationship. In Exodus 17, the Israelites are fighting with Moses because they want water. Moses cries out to the Lord, "What am I to do with these people?" (v. 4). You've probably asked God that same question about your husband. Take heart—the Lord answers Moses with specific instructions in the next verse. He'll answer your prayer too.

See your husband's point of view. Play the scene from his perspective. During a disagreement, I've thought, *I don't like you very much.* I've turned it around and realized he probably doesn't like me either. After all, what have I done lately to endear myself to him? That puts things in perspective, doesn't it? Instead of focusing on what your spouse did to offend you, be mindful of the ways you may have offended him.

Remind yourself that silence is golden. Have you ever yelled at your husband in the heat of the moment only to regret it later? Has your husband spoken harsh words to you that are lodged in your heart and memory? "Sticks and stones may break my bones, but words will never hurt me" just isn't true. It's the hateful words spoken between partners that resurface years later in front of a marriage counselor. If you can't say anything constructive, walk away from the situation until you can.

On a Focus on the Family webcast, *Love and Respect* author Emerson Eggerichs gave this advice: "Ask your husband, 'Did I say or do something that felt disrespectful to you?' And go quiet. What you've done is spoken on his honor code—it would soften him. Just like if he said to you, 'Did that feel unloving?' That would soften you. The more mature person initiates."[19]

Say what's in your heart. After you've sought God, considered your husband's point of view, and cooled off, you're ready to talk. Don't let things fester under the guise of keeping peace in the family. Your husband needs to know what's bothering you. He's not a mind reader. You'll explode like my oatmeal if you let things go too long.

My boss when I worked at *The 700 Club,* Andy Freeman, says this about his wife, Teresa:

> In thirty years of marriage, we've had our disagreements and debates but never in a way that would embarrass or hurt one another. We have never raised our voices or entered a shouting match with one another. Now, I am prone to sarcasm (the dark side of humor), and Teresa can "run silent, run deep" like a submarine. But by giving each other a bit of time and space, we always have been able to find resolution and support for each other.[20]

The Cup of Kindness

Early in Mark Matlock's marriage, he traveled extensively speaking to youth. The rhythm of his married life was constantly changing. He and his wife, Jade, kept waiting for that perfect time to talk, but those times rarely happened. They decided to create a monthly "state of the family" meeting. During that time, they went over finances, reviewed the calendar, and talked about things that were problematic. Mark said:

> Rather than these conversations popping up in the middle of the day and stressing everything out, it was in your mind that on a certain day of the month, we're actually going to have a conversation about this. Things that might have blown up in the past became maintenance issues. It was like a garden that needed to be tended rather than something that needed to be built. [21]

There's no question in my mind that having in place a system to talk significantly reduces arguments and tension. But, of course, we're all human, and sparks can fly even with the best-laid plans. I like one of Jade's remedies and her great perspective:

> There are times when I'm irritated at Mark, and I have to make a conscious decision to turn the day in a positive way. Our evening could go one way or another. It goes against my flesh to show him love. I focus on something good and try to do something loving. My heart changes, and he's happy and I'm happy. [22]

For Jade, one of those loving acts is brewing a cup of tea for Mark. This requires some sacrifice since he prefers loose-leaf tea, so it takes more effort than just dunking a tea bag in hot water. She doesn't enjoy preparing it or drinking it. She's a coffee girl. But she goes through the rigmarole of making the tea. Why? She does it out of love even when she's irritated.

So the next time you feel irritated at your husband, you might just want to grab a cup and brew some tea.

Notice Today:

How often do you argue with your husband?

Seldom   Weekly

Sometimes   Daily or almost daily

What are most of your disagreements with your husband about?

Nurture Today:

The next time you experience conflict with your husband, go quiet. Not "ice princess" quiet but "I want to try to understand you" quiet. Treat your husband with respect and value his opinion the same way you want your opinion valued.

Day 11

Cue the Knight

My beloved is radiant and ruddy,
outstanding among ten thousand.

Song of Songs 5:10

One of the first movies I saw with James when we were just friends was *Princess Bride*. The movie is a classic love story between the beautiful Buttercup and her beloved Westley, who she believes was killed. But Westley is not dead; he has in fact returned as the Dread Pirate Roberts to rescue Buttercup from marrying Prince Humperdinck.

> *Westley*: I told you I would always come for you. Why didn't you wait for me?
>
> *Buttercup*: Well…you were dead.
>
> *Westley*: Death cannot stop true love. All it can do is delay it for a while.
>
> *Buttercup*: I will never doubt again.
>
> *Westley*: There will never be a need. [23]

At this point in the movie, I looked over at James, who had declared our relationship to be merely platonic. But I saw in him my Westley, my true love. Sometimes you have to wait for your knight to figure out that you're the right damsel in distress.

James and I eventually found true love, and so did you with your husband. Is he still your knight in shining armor? Epic movies like *Braveheart* and *Gladiator* celebrate men who can duel to the death and win the heart of a princess. Husbands want to be warriors fighting for the welfare of their families, sweeping their wives off their feet and rescuing their children.

The Hercules in Your Home

For six seasons, Kevin Sorbo starred as Hercules on one of the highest-rated syndicated shows in television history, *Hercules: The Legendary Journeys*. He and his wife met on the set of Hercules. Kevin says,

> I understand that romantic side of being single, but there are pros and cons with all that stuff. I find much more joy in having children and raising them. My wife, Sam, and I just had our thirteenth anniversary. I said to Sam, "That's like a silver anniversary in Hollywood."[24]

You don't have to talk with Kevin very long to find out he's crazy about his three young children Braeden, Shane, and Octavia. He saves their messages on his phone so he'll be able listen to them decades from now. He writes down the funny things they say. He cherishes his morning time with each child as they wake up (Kevin is the early riser of the family). Kevin doesn't agree with Hollywood's portrayal of today's husband and father.

> Men want to be reassured that they're the man of the family. Hollywood does such a great job of demasculinizing men. If you look at any sitcom, that guy's an idiot. He's a moron. His kids are all rolling their eyes. They've done that for decades. Kids grow up watching that, and they think fathers are idiots. It's the mom that can do anything and she's a babe on top of it. They do that a lot in shows. It's ridiculous. You look before with *Father Knows Best* or *My Three Sons*, the dad had smart things to say to his kids. He was a moral man who led by good example. For some reason, it's become funny to make the dad fat and stupid.[25]

Wives, we have the power to turn this stereotype around in our homes, making our husbands feel more like Hercules and less like Homer Simpson.

Movie Moments, Mundane Moments

Most days aren't filled with movie moments: Westley declaring his undying love to Buttercup; Hercules saving villagers from evil warlords. The average day is a series of rather mundane moments ranging from driving to work, checking emails, making kids do homework, and cooking dinner.

Mark Matlock has been working with youth pastors, students, and parents for more than two decades. He's the executive director at Youth Specialties, founder of WisdomWorks Ministries, and author of several books, including *Real World Parents* and *Freshman*. But in my book, his claim to fame is that he cooks dinner for his family of four whenever he's not traveling.

After their kids were born, Mark noticed dinnertime was very stressful for his wife, Jade. He decided to step in and take that responsibility off her plate. That freed up extra time and energy for Jade to be more relaxed and conversational (and Jade adds quickly that cooking is therapy for Mark). Mark also says he's realizing more and more just how much Jade does around the home.

> I think women's retreats were completely designed to make men realize what women really go through when they're at home. I remember when I had to get my daughter Skye's hair ready before we went to church. I was like, "Oh no. I can't do this. There's too much." The house was just a wreck because I didn't realize how much Jade is cleaning up all the time. *Holy cow, did I make all this mess?*[26]

Wives, you do a lot around the house that often goes unnoticed until you're not there to do it. But guess what? So does your man. Whether he's cooking dinner (my James has graduated from pizza bagels to chicken), changing the oil in the car, putting the kids to bed, or paying bills online, he could use a heartfelt "thank you."

You're My Superman

Patrick Brown, host of TLC's *Home Made Simple,* talks about the power of his wife to make him feel like a hero:

> People joke about celebrities saying, "Who do you think you are? God's gift to the world?" My wife really does make me feel like I'm God's gift to her and the world. She actually says those

things with her mouth. That makes a man feel different. A wife can show her husband an unwavering belief that God has called him to his station in life. If a woman can get in her mind that what her husband is doing is the same thing that Superman is doing when he's holding a train back from falling over a cliff, that makes a man feel like there's nothing he wouldn't do when he gets home. [27]

A few years ago, my family planned a camping trip that was the same day as the annual air show in our town. Ethan was playing with a toy jet, and I mentioned casually, "Oh, we won't be able to go to the air show this year because we'll be camping."

He erupted. "I want to go to the air show. Can't we go camping another time?"

I put him on my lap and let him cry. I couldn't find a way to console him. The flood of tears turned into a terribly testy mood, and I'm not sure which was worse.

James came home, and when he found out what was going on, he took Ethan into his room. A few minutes later, Ethan emerged a totally different little boy. I'm not sure all that took place between those two, but sometimes when a kid throws a fit, there's nothing like talking it out with his father.

Maybe you're a little discouraged because your husband hasn't been acting much like Hercules, Superman, or Super Daddy lately. Why don't you talk to your heavenly Father about it?

Today's reading began with a scene from *Princess Bride*. Toward the end of the movie, Westley is nearly dead after being tortured by Prince Humperdinck. Desperate for help, his friends bring him to Miracle Max for a cure. They're in quite a hurry, to which Miracle Max replies, "You rush a miracle man, you get rotten miracles."

Your knight husband may be taking his time swooping you off into the sunset. But don't rush your miracle. Bring your cares to God, who is infinitely more trustworthy than Miracle Max, and wait for your knight.

Notice Today:

What attributes of royalty does your husband possess? This month, when you see that attribute in action, notice.

Nurture Today:

Kiss your prince tenderly today. Kiss him when he arrives home. Kiss him whether he has good news, bad news, or no news. Kiss him and tell him that you appreciate that he is _____ (and fill in the attribute you noted above).

Guide 3

Domestic Tranquillity

Respect

Eros
Your husband needs a fulfilling sex life.

Attraction

Mutual Activities

Day 12

Numero Uno

It is better to marry than to burn with passion.

1 Corinthians 7:9

Since we've been talking about respect, I asked James how I can better show him respect. His answer surprised me. I thought he would thank me for speaking well of him to others. Instead he told me to show my respect in the bedroom.

In the bedroom?

James in his own words sheds light on the subject of sex and its close connection for many men to respect:

> Whatever your man's need is, you have to respect that. And if you don't, you don't respect your guy. The joke in the church among guys is we got married and we burn more now than we did before we got married. Is that respect? It's a misalignment in the woman's mind of what's important. She feels she has to clean the kitchen, clean the floor, help the kids with the homework, and the guy's dying. The guy feels entitled. When people feel entitled, they do bad things. If a man feels he's been dieting and dieting sexually, he's going to check out some eye candy. And it all boils down to a lack of respect.

> Very few men are going to share this with their wives. They're just going to sweep it under the rug, and the next thing you know they have marriage problems. And it all stems from the lack of respect by discounting one of his valid needs.

What need does your man have that perhaps you have discounted? It may be sex or it may be something else. Your husband has a dreamy idea of what your marriage could be like too. He may long for more quality time, the cookies you used to bake him, going to ball games together again, or a half-naked wife to greet him at the door. You have the power and privilege of making his dreams come true.

His Number One Need

James and I attend a parenting class at our church. I had the opportunity to ask the husbands in the class to list their top five needs in marriage. The wives were instructed to predict what those top five needs would be. The secondary needs varied, but the number one need was the same at every single table. Numero uno: sexual fulfillment. No big surprise, yet why are so many wives struggling to meet this basic need in our men?

I think part of the answer lies in the many things we do right. Other needs that were identified were:

- Affirmation
- Meaningful conversation
- Shared interests and activities
- Appearance
- Friendship
- Calm and peaceful home

Maybe you're doing pretty well on this checklist. You endured an action flick, went to the gym, took care of the kids, and even put on lipstick before he came home from work. Doesn't all that count for something? Compared to the other wives you know, you're actually quite considerate. Yet you may be discounting his number one need. Odds are your husband wants you to make fulfilling sex the top priority in your marriage.

A Broken Tile

Imagine buying a new home. You find a house you love except in the bathroom one of the tiles is badly cracked in the shower. Would you overlook the damaged tile? After all, there are dozens of perfectly good tiles in the shower too. No, you would ask for that tile to be replaced. Left broken, the tile would be a major eyesore and a potential source of water damage. After being repaired, it wouldn't be an issue at all, merely blending in with all the other tiles.

Your sex life is like that broken tile. When your husband isn't satisfied, he is totally fixated on that broken tile. All his energy goes into getting that tile repaired. And if he can't fix it, after a while he gives up. Now he's resentful every time he looks at it. On the other hand, if he's able to fix it, he's golden. The tile is no longer an issue.

It's time to fix the sex tile in our marriages. Too many marital unions are ruined because women (and men) write off the importance of sexual happiness. The first step of restoration is found in 1 Corinthians 7:2-4:

> Since sexual immorality is occurring, each man should have sexual relations with his own wife, and each woman with her own husband. The husband should fulfill his marital duty to his wife, and likewise the wife to her husband. The wife does not have authority over her own body but yields it to her husband. In the same way, the husband does not have authority over his own body but yields it to his wife.

Notice the reciprocal nature of this passage. Your husband doesn't want sex to only be about meeting his needs, as if he's a sex-crazed animal. He wants to meet your sexual needs too. Remember when you were engaged? You looked forward to making love to your new husband. It's time to go back to that first love when you were as interested in being intimate as he was.

David Clarke suggests having a regular dialogue with your husband about your sex life. Ask each other, *What can I do better? What would you like from me?* Sex happens spontaneously and passionately on the big screen but rarely in real life if you're a busy person. Dr. Clarke suggests,

> Working as a team, you schedule your sex. If you have kids and you don't schedule sex, you don't have sex. Or at least you don't have it very often. Here's how it works. If we schedule that we're going to have sex in one or two days, we can both start getting prepared. The man doesn't need much time, but the woman does. Now she can start looking forward to it and marshaling her resources so she's not spent that day. That's a day that you want to save your energy and start thinking about it. Women have to

work on this more than men. We think about sex all the time. Now we think about it with our wives, that's the good news.[1]

When you start talking about sex with your man, putting it on your calendar and making sure it happens, that broken tile will be fixed in no time.

The Currency of Appreciation

One day I asked James, "Why is sex so important to a man?"

He thought about the question and then came back a few hours later with this story. When he was a teenager, he worked at a country club. Many times when he had gone the extra mile for a guest, he would receive a nice tip. On the flip side, others who received the same level of service would just say thanks without the tip. It wasn't about dollars and cents. It was about someone appreciating his service and showing that appreciation through the tip.

James then said, "It's the action of sex that makes me feel really appreciated."

I realized in that moment that sex is the currency of appreciation for many men. Wives feel appreciated emotionally. Husbands feel appreciated physically. Your husband needs not only the words, "I appreciate you." He needs actions to back it up. And that, my friend, is one way to show respect.

Notice Today:

Go back to the night before your wedding day. How did you dream about making love to your husband? Think about how you felt about him and how you desired his touch.

Nurture Today:

Now is the time to make that dream come true again. Plan a romantic evening with your spouse. When you make love, remember in your mind how lucky you felt on your wedding day.

Day 13

Free to Be Me

I am faint with love.

SONG OF SONGS 2:5

When we were engaged, James and I were given the classic best-selling book, *The Gift of Sex: A Guide to Sexual Fulfillment* by Cliff and Joyce Penner. That 1981 edition had already sold 250,000 copies, so you can imagine the influence of their writing today. When I had the opportunity to interview the Penners for this book, you can only imagine my excitement.[2]

My first question was, "I know men typically would like to have more sex in the marriage, so how can a woman cultivate her appetite for sex?"

Their response got my attention.

"We might see it a little different than most people see it," Joyce said. "We would ask a different question. We think that a woman will get with her sexuality and her desire when that doesn't come as a demand or a pressure from the husband. Men are trying to get it in the wrong way."

"As he adores her and compliments her, connecting with her heart, then she is able to open up her body," Cliff said. "There is nothing that turns on a man more than a turned-on woman."

Instead of being sexually turned on for her *husband*, the Penners help women learn how to be sexually turned on for *themselves*. After thirty-five years as sexual therapists and forty-eight years of marriage, the Penners believe this is clearly what works. Cliff says,

> Men are trying to get her to do it for him. We're trying to get her
> to the place where the woman is doing it for herself. When she

is truly into it for herself, he will be happy. There is no question about that. If you have any doubt about that, just think about the pornography industry. The porn industry is all about the woman behaving as if she loves it.

Joyce adds,

Unfortunately most men think if they could just get her into more recreational sex, then he would be happy. But the more she tries to do that, the more pressure there is on her. The more she tries to do it for him, the less she is into it for herself. The less she is into for herself, the less turned-on she is. The less turned-on she is, the less happy he is.

Intensely Sexual?

So if the goal is being a turned-on woman, what if your man isn't giving you a whole lot to get turned on about? Then the greatest gift you can give to your husband is to get in touch with and live out your sexual self.

"The wife has to believe that one, she is a sexual person, and two, it is her right to be intensely sexual," Cliff says. Joyce explains further that the biggest challenge working with women is helping them become sexually "selfish," embracing their own sexuality as God designed:

The woman has the only body part, the clitoris, that has no other purpose than to transmit and receive sexual stimulation. When we understand how the woman's body works during sexual arousal and release, there are changes that are only designed for the purpose of pleasure that happen in the body.

One of the games we women play is to think, *If he really loved me, he'd do this and do that,* rather than taking responsibility for ourselves and understanding when is it that we've had the best times sexually? What makes it the best? What can I do to make sure that happens? How can I prepare for that?

Many women have false expectations about themselves and their husbands, whether it's from having read romance novels, watching movies, or having previous sexual experience before marriage. They are looking for what we call dopamine-driven sex, the adrenaline sex that just zaps you and overtakes you. If you don't feel those kinds of feelings, you think, *He just doesn't turn me on*, and you shut down. Married sex doesn't function on that kind of romance-novel type of response. It functions on a much deeper, connected intimacy.

Turn Me On

So how do you become more in tune with your sexuality? Often Christian women think of the sexually turned-on woman as a negative stereotype. That's not too surprising considering the media rarely depicts a sexy woman in a fulfilling monogamous relationship.

When Ethan was two, he ate a cashew and broke out in hives. We concluded he was allergic to nuts and trained him from a young age to avoid eating them. A few years later, we tested a few nuts on him with surprising results. He's eaten a peanut, pistachio, almond, and even a cashew again with no symptoms at all. Now we tell him, "It's okay if you want to try a nut while Mommy and Daddy are with you." But Ethan is so programmed to avoid nuts, he doesn't want to indulge himself, even when offered a yummy cinnamon roll topped with pecans.

Christian women can view sex like that nut allergy. For much of our lives, we've been programmed to avoid thinking about sex and having sex. Sex is something to avoid, not something to crave. After marriage, these prohibitions still occupy our minds even though the marriage license says sex is now okay. So the first thing to do is give yourself permission to get turned on. God created you as a sexual being.

One thing you can do to enhance your sexual experience is Kegel exercises. You may remember doing them after childbirth. To do a Kegel exercise, you pretend as though you are trying to stop and then release the flow of urine. This pelvic-floor exercise can be done while sitting at the computer (yes, I just did one), washing dishes, or brushing your teeth. When you strengthen your pelvic floor, it enhances sexual enjoyment for you and your husband and also helps you fight incontinence.

Start by doing three sets of ten Kegel exercises daily. To take it to the next level, purchase small Kegel vaginal weights to help you strengthen your pelvic floor even more effectively. When your husband sees a package arrive in the mail with a Kegel exercise product inside, it will send a very positive message. Kind of like if you found a bunch of "Improve Your Marriage by Pampering Your Wife" books in his mail pile.

Keep learning about your sexuality by reading books and articles from reputable sources. Choose books like *The Gift of Sex*, *The Act of Marriage* by Tim and Beverly LaHaye, and *Red-Hot Monogamy* by Bill and Pam Farrel. Read a chapter aloud to each other in bed. It works great when the husband reads a chapter about what sex means to a woman, and you read aloud what sex means to a man. Be sure to leave some time for the lab afterwards. Remember, your focus is not on how to twist yourself into a new sexual position. It's about being free, alive, and comfortable with your sexuality.

Lastly, don't forget that deepening your sexuality with your spouse is fun. Take the pressure off yourself to be perfect.

A few years ago, I read about being more creative in bed and trying belly dancing. Lord knows I can't do that, but what I did was make up my own dance of the seven veils. I layered myself in four silk scarves, two swimsuit cover-ups, and one winter scarf. I hardly looked like a seductress; I looked more like a mixed-up bag lady. But I charged into the room and pretended to be a belly dancer. My husband didn't lust, he laughed, and we had a great night together. Free to be me.

Notice Today:

Do you agree with the Penners that "nothing turns on a man like a turned-on woman?"

Nurture Today:

What's something concrete you can do this week to get more turned on sexually? Reading a book aloud with your husband? Kegel exercises? Taking the pressure off mentally?

Day 14

Garlic Killed My Love Life

The husband should fulfill his wife's sexual needs,
and the wife should fulfill her husband's needs.

1 CORINTHIANS 7:3 (NLT)

When you're pregnant with your third child, sex isn't usually high on the priority list. Sleep and chocolate are. But one strange day when I was about thirteen-weeks pregnant, I was actually looking forward to some romance on a Friday night. Earlier in the day, my highlight had been devouring pita chips and garlic hummus.

I changed my clothes and got ready for my evening of romance. James walked in, and as he drew close, he stopped dead in his tracks.

"What is that smell?"

It took two seconds to figure out it was my beloved garlic hummus.

"I can smell you and that garlic in every room," he moaned.

I apologized and winked.

He hesitated and replied, "I don't know if I can handle your breath."

You probably know what happened next. Nothing. Absolutely nothing. My breath was the deal killer. After he talked himself into plugging his nose and taking the plunge, I was no longer in the mood. Romance dies quickly after any kind of confrontation involving Listerine.

Whether it's bad breath, a headache, that time of the month, or hot flashes, something often gets in the way of romance. Sometimes it's your spouse, sometimes it's you. How can a couple overcome these roadblocks to intimacy in a respectful way that doesn't offend either partner?

I Don't Really Have a Headache

It's the classic bedroom scene of the couple that's been married for a few years. The husband inches toward his wife in bed and gives her the look. She sighs and says, "I'm sorry, dear. I have a headache and just don't feel like myself."

From a wife's perspective, she's thinking, *Please leave me alone. I just want to go to bed.* It isn't meant to be an insult to her husband.

From what I've heard, many men are thinking, *You've been having a lot of headaches lately. I don't think you care about me anymore.*

Radio talk-show host Dennis Prager, in an article titled "When a Woman Isn't in the Mood: Part 1," encourages the wife to rethink the axiom that if she's not in the mood, she doesn't have to make love to her husband.

> Women need to recognize how a man understands a wife's refusal to have sex with him: A husband knows that his wife loves him first and foremost by her willingness to give her body to him. This is rarely the case for women. A man whose wife frequently denies him sex will first be hurt, then sad, then angry, then quiet. And most men will never tell their wives why they have become quiet and distant. They are afraid to tell their wives.[3]

If your husband became quiet and distant, wouldn't you want to know what was going on? And if he told you he was upset about the lack of sex in your marriage, how would you respond?

Too often women blame their mood when it comes to making love. If you wait until you are in the mood to go to work, head to the gym, or change your baby's diaper, you might be sitting on the couch for quite some time. Every day, you decide to behave in ways that go against your mood. Yet somehow when it comes to sex, mood trumps everything else.

Sex in Boots

I sprained my ankle badly last year and wore a big black boot up to my knee. I wasn't bathing every day and had greasy hair because I was planning to get a haircut later that day. My kids had gone over to my parents to give me time to write. Three words described my state: gimpy, greasy, gross.

In walked Casanova with a dozen white roses. It was such a sweet gesture. A little bit later, James walked up to my desk and asked if, you know, we had time for "wink wink." I could have said I felt too gross. I could have reminded him that this was the first time I had been able to write in days. But instead I said, "How about in a half hour?"

Did I feel sensuous wearing my clunky black ankle boot? Did I feel attractive with my greasy hair? Did I want to have sex instead of getting some work done? Not really. Did it make sense to make time for sex? Definitely. It had been a long time since we were alone in the house without the kids. I found out that if you do the right thing, your mood will follow your behavior. Besides, don't people say black boots are sexy?

It's Not the Boot, It's...

What's killing your love life lately? Since it's probably not garlic or a big black boot, maybe you're struggling with one of the following.

I am hurt by something my husband said. While it's true our husbands can say things that require a grand apology, many times they unwittingly hit a hot button or say something small that gets blown out of proportion. When James asks, "What have you been doing all day?" that makes my blood boil. I have to learn how to snap out of the defensive mode and answer the question calmly. (By the way, I have instructed him not to use this question anymore.)

I am exhausted, really. You have pressures with your work, caring for family members, and keeping your household running. Those nights when you can barely brush your teeth, let alone make love to your husband, will come. Do your best to carve out time each week for lovemaking when you're not so tired.

I am preoccupied with all I have to do. When your head hits the pillow, you're not thinking what would feel best sexually. You're thinking of how you're going to deal with that difficult person at work, what you're going to wear to the party, and how you're going to get to the grocery store tomorrow since the schedule's so tight. A place to jot your thoughts down before bed may help silence that nagging to-do list.

From Duty to Decision

Should a wife have sex with her husband out of duty or obligation? Joyce Penner offers a helpful answer to this question.

> We like sex best when we have the desire for it. But there are stages in life when we won't have the desire for it, like when the

kids are young and we're exhausted. Duty sex and demand sex never work. When you do it out of obligation, it may work for tonight but not long term. But sex by *decision* can work, and there's a big difference.

Duty says, "I know he needs it. He's a man. It's been seven days. But I'm tired and I don't feel like it." That's duty sex, and it's not going to work. Sex by decision says, "You know what, it's been seven days. I know I need it, and I know we need it. Let's make a plan for how we can make it the best for both of us." It's got to be as good for her as it is for him if it's going to work for a lifetime.

Wives need to design life so we can get with the program sexually rather than saying I need to put out even when I'm exhausted because he needs it. That will never work.[4]

When you make the decision to honor your marriage bed, both you and your husband will benefit sexually. So the next time garlic, stress, mood, or anything else threatens your love life, make the switch from duty to decision and go for it.

Notice Today:

Has your husband hinted lately that he wants to have sex? How did you respond? Do you think your husband feels free to initiate lovemaking or does he "know better"?

Nurture Today:

The next time you're not in the mood to have sex, remember this chapter. Make the decision to invest in your marriage sexually, and let your feelings follow your actions.

Day 15

Clear and Present Danger

All at once he followed her…
like a bird darting into a snare,
little knowing it will cost him his life.
PROVERBS 7:22-23

More than ever before, pornography threatens your family. Sex therapist and clinical psychologist Cliff Penner has counseled couples for thirty-five years and says, "Porn is a giant issue. It used to be if you wanted to get pornography, you had to go to that seedy bookstore in the trashy part of town. Now it's on every computer. You get to it whether you want it or not."[5]

Consider these shocking statistics about Internet pornography:

- 12% of the websites on the Internet are pornographic

- 42.7% of Internet users view porn

- 70% of men aged 18-24 visit porn sites in a typical month

- 25% of all search engine requests are pornography related (that's 68 million a day)

- 34% of Internet users have experienced unwanted exposure to porn either through pop-up ads, misdirected links or emails

- 53% of Promise Keeper men viewed porn in the last week

- 47% of Christians say porn is a major problem in the home[6]

If you think you or your husband can't fall prey to porn, think again. It really could happen to anyone.

Sam's Story

When Sam was in fifth grade, he was left alone at a friend's house. His friend said, "Let's play with our pee-pees," and Sam's sex education formally began. Porn wasn't available as it is today. Sam fantasized about teachers who wore low-cut blouses or underwear models in the Sears catalog. In high school, he masturbated regularly in the bathroom. His sex drive consumed him, and there was no shutting it down. In college, he got to play out his fantasies with a different woman at every party.

After graduating, Sam continued his sexual conquests and pursued acting. One day an acting buddy asked him, "Sam, are you sick and tired of hurting?" Thinking that was a strange question but desperately wanting to get out of the cycle of sexual addiction, he agreed to meet his friend's spiritual mentor. Sam said,

> I knew I needed to get out of the life that was destroying me, so I did exactly what he instructed: I called him and prayed daily; I fasted from food once a week; I attended weekly group meetings. But the harder I tried to deny myself, the stronger the cravings became. There was only one thing to do—get married.[7]

Enter Maria, who married her knight in shining armor, never knowing about Sam's addiction to pornography. Neither were Christians at the time. When she discovered the truth of Sam's hard-core addiction, Maria was blown away. In the next year or two, she watched him like a hawk. She saw his failings, but she also saw his brokenness as he often cried and pleaded to God for deliverance. Finally, one Sunday morning, they visited a church and the Holy Spirit spoke to them both. They committed their lives to Christ. But change didn't happen overnight. For the next few years, Sam spent plenty of nights on the sofa or getting his clothes thrown out on the front yard.

> Maria was basically a sacrificial lamb. When we would walk into a restaurant, my head was whipping from side to side checking out everything there was. When the waitress came over, I was

flirting with her. It was my nature and it had to just kill her. But
she never kept sex from me and she had to be hurting.[8]

Maria heard a speaker say something that became her mantra in a trou-
bled marriage: *Submission is ducking low enough so God can deck him.* One
creative way God decked Sam was through a bunch of rowdy kids. At
Maria's prompting, Sam started serving and helping with the junior-high
group at their church. Every three weeks, Sam had to give the message,
and he realized if he was sinning sexually, he wouldn't be able to stand in
front of those boys and girls with a clear conscience. Knowing that a group
of kids was counting on him was a big part of Sam's healing.

Another milestone was having a baby daughter. "When she was born,
I was a changed man. It helped me incredibly with my selfishness because
I would do anything for that girl. I started to realize that all of the women
in porn were somebody's little girl." That contributed to the end of pornography in Sam's life.

> I have never met a man that was deeper into sexual sin than I was.
> My roommate died of AIDS in the early eighties; I partied with
> these guys. I thought I would take it to my grave, but I cried out
> to God and said, "I want You to break me. I don't care if You take
> an arm, if You take an eye, whatever it takes, just do it." By the
> mercy of God He gave me victory. I can't imagine a man who
> truly wants to be free, and God not allowing him to be free.[9]

Sam has been married for twenty-three years now. He hasn't looked at
pornography since 1995 and is incredibly thankful that he broke his addiction before all the technology available today.

Get Your War Paint On

How can you know when your husband is being tempted by pornography? Sam said if he finds himself fighting the urge to look at women, he
wonders how long has it been since he's been intimate with his wife. The
red flag goes up, and he tells Maria, "We need to have a date."

What does that tell us wives? When your husband wants some action
in the bedroom, don't rationalize it away and put it off too long. Your husband can rationalize just as well, justifying pornography as a way to get
relief and pleasure since you're not engaging. Sam says,

The wife needs to know, once her husband has gotten into this area, I believe it is Satan's main domain. You're talking about spiritual warfare that is unbelievable. You turn on that computer at home and turn on a pornographic website, you have just ushered demons into your home. The only way to fight that is through Jesus Christ. You've got to get praying and wisely choose some good people to pray with you.[10]

Cliff Penner says you've got to have the hedges up at home and on your man's electronics (if you're the one struggling with porn, this applies to you):

Begin by accepting there's no way he's going to manage this by himself without outside help. You can ask him, "How many times have you prayed for forgiveness for this?" Oh, about a thousand. "How many times have you said I'm not going to do this again?" Oh, about a thousand. "It hasn't changed, has it?" This will help him see he is helpless to deal with it by himself.

Then manage the home. Protect the computers and go to bed at the same time. Most of the time this stuff happens after the wife goes to bed. The wife should have all the passwords, and the computer should face so everyone can see it. Lastly, have a support group and accountability partner.[11]

If pornography is poisoning your marriage, this is not the time to give up. Get your war paint on, sister, and fight fire with fire. You have something very important a porn star can never give your husband, and that's love. Dave Carder talks about oxytocin, the hormone involved in birth and lactation, trust and bonding, and sexual arousal:

Women will have the highest spikes of oxytocin when they are nursing. Male spikes of oxytocin occur only when you have sex with someone who loves you. You have an elevation but not a major spike when you have sex with prostitutes and when you masturbate. So guys who are into porn, habitually masturbating, seeing prostitutes, and going to strip clubs, they're settling for little tiny elevations of oxytocin. They won't be satisfied; they never will.[12]

Give your husband so much loving at home that he doesn't have the sexual need or energy to look elsewhere. You want to take care of each other.

Notice Today:

Are you comfortable talking about pornography with your husband? Do you think it is a concern in your marriage?

Nurture Today:

If porn is a concern, make a commitment together to work through the above steps outlined by Dr. Penner. Show your husband this week that you want to turn on the heat at home.

Day 16

Stranger in the Night

Come together again so that Satan will not tempt
you because of your lack of self-control.

1 Corinthians 7:5

Seth and Nancy seemed like the perfectly happy Christian couple. Married for more than thirty years, they had raised successful children. They served in leadership in their local church and gave their time and talents to missions. No one could have seen it coming when Seth had an affair, not even his wife.

We all know people like Seth and Nancy. Whether their story strikes close to home, it's wise to recognize that an affair could happen in any marriage. David Frisbie counsels many couples struggling with infidelity and says,

> It is so easy to stray now. You can find a person with two clicks of the mouse. I think anything that a woman can do to keep her husband satisfied and taken care of will help. I hate to say that out loud because it sounds like I'm putting the burden on a woman, like it's all her fault that the sexuality doesn't work. I would not go to any of those places. I just think strategically as a wife, if you can keep your husband physically satisfied, that's a wonderful thing to do.[13]

Smart and Savvy

So how can you be smart about your husband's sexuality and savvy about your own? Bill Farrel, coauthor with his wife, Pam, of *Red-Hot Monogamy*, says,

> We all talk about a woman's cycle, but there's a cycle that men go through too. Every three or four days, a man's body gets ready to have sex. There are times when guys don't think straight, they don't feel straight, and they are just grumpy and irritable until they can have sex. As soon as they have sex, they look at the world differently. A guy who's married to a wife that will accept that and say, "I'm going to help you do better by sometimes having sex just because you want to"—those men are madly in love with those women because they can't believe she actually understands.[14]

Many years ago, Bill had to attend a conference of mostly women. He put on a good front, but he dreaded going. Without Bill having a clue, Pam had arranged for a friend to watch the kids. She arrived at the hotel while he was at dinner with colleagues. When he returned to his room, grumbling about the terrible time he was having, imagine his surprise to find his beautiful wife, a candlelit room, and homemade chocolate-chip cookies. "She set up this whole clandestine affair, and we had a great night together. She got up early the next morning to drive home to be with the kids. I'm sure she was exhausted all day, but that day lives on forever," Bill says.

That's the kind of affair that's good for a marriage. If we can create memorable meetings like that once in a while, those moments will be well worth the planning. Here's something else Pam does to keep Bill close to her heart that you can try too.

> If I'm gone for a few days or really busy at work, Pam will actually go through my closet and put on shirts of mine. She'll find one that has my cologne on it. She'll just take time and smell it. She'll pause in the middle of the day and think about times we've been together that she really enjoyed. It warms her up to the whole idea of intimacy. Pam deliberately cultivates her appetite for us to be together sexually.[15]

What If I Want Sex More Than He Does?

You may be the one in the marriage who has more interest in sex. What if he is intimidated by sex or by intimacy? What if he sees your sexual needs as pressure? In their practice, Cliff and Joyce Penner observe that of those couples reporting desire issues, 60 percent are there because the wife lacks sexual desire and 40 percent are there because of the husband's lack of desire. How can you best communicate your desire for more physical intimacy without alienating or intimidating your husband? Joyce suggests having a conversation that goes something like this:

> Sex is really important to me and our marriage is really important to me. What I sense from you is that you just don't feel the urge or desire as often as I do. That leaves me kind of hanging. I want to honor your level of desire, but I also want us to stay connected sexually. How can we work this out?

Cliff adds,

> The woman needs to be empathetic of where he is and also to speak the truth about where she is—to say, I'm not against you; in fact, I want more of you. It's an affirming message that sends care and support and understanding. We as men can be pretty sensitive if we get the message, "You're not measuring up sexually, buddy," so that's why it has to be in a message of support, care, and empathy.[16]

David Frisbie also adds that a wife can be sensitive toward when her husband is most receptive to having sex.

> She's going to simply have to take her cues from the husband. It's unlikely that her attempts to be provocative are going to be successful, although it could happen. Much better is to catch him when he's already in that mood. You can tell when there's a receptive moment. You can also tell when a receptive moment is moving forward. It's much better to pay attention to him rather than plan out something in your mind of, *I'm going to be all seductive and wear this.* Those efforts often end in frustration.[17]

Three Ways to Affair Proof Your Marriage

After working for many years with couples caught in adultery, Dave Carder has identified three powerful ways to protect your marriage.

> *1. Have fun.* I think the critical thing is most people get married because they had fun together. They stop having fun when they start having kids. You need to go back to fun. Usually in most marriages, one spouse is more fun-loving than the other one. If it happens to be the husband that's fun-loving, oftentimes the wife doesn't respect him. You've got to build fun, individual and

joint fun, into the relationship. In this culture, if you don't plan and build fun into your marriage, there won't be fun. Then you'll find somebody else to have fun with. I think rituals are a huge part of maintaining attraction. A ritual is something you antic- ipate doing that if it doesn't happen, you're both disappointed.

2. Build sexual tension. Many men ruin their wives because every time there was flirting, he took her up to bed to have sex. She didn't want that. She wanted the teasing, the flirting, and hav- ing fun. I tell guys in premarital counseling, you need to put off the sexual experience and create sexual tension between the two of you. Sexual tension is what you wanted to do when you were dating but you couldn't do. You need to create that sexual tension again between the two of you through notes, texting, emails, etc.

3. Admit attraction. If you find yourself attracted to somebody else, and you will unless you're dead or in denial, you need to talk about that openly. If there's an attraction, you need to figure out, what is it that creates this attraction? What does this high- light that we need to do more of? Why is this person appealing? You need to talk about this in a safe environment without your spouse getting angry. Now if you're bringing up a friendship or attraction every week, you're crazy. You've got another problem. But it may happen sporadically.[18]

Even if the conversations get awkward, resolve to use every experience in life for the good and growth of your marriage. You don't want the old Frank Sinatra song "Stranger in the Night" to have anything to do with your love story.

Notice Today:

How are you and your husband doing in the areas of having fun, building sexual tension, and attraction to others?

Nurture Today:

Have fun flirting with your husband today. Hide love notes throughout the house. Text him about how you want his body.

From Sunday School to the Locker Room

A loving doe, a graceful deer—
may her breasts satisfy you always,
may you ever be intoxicated with her love.

PROVERBS 5:19

M en talk to each other about sex. They made jokes about it in the junior-high locker room and it's still the hot topic of conversation today. Women, especially Christian women, don't chat about sex. We talk about kids, mothers-in-law, recipes, clothes, and feelings. I can count on one hand the conversations I've had in the last decade with friends about sex. I know that may not be true of other women, but men generally talk about sex a whole lot more than women do.

In his men's Bible study, my friend Steven asked, "Who has masturbated?" Considering that these men were ushers, deacons, and leaders in the church who had been married thirty plus years, he thought it would be zero. Turns out five out of the six men said they masturbated. These are married men active in church life, and *they* are struggling to have their sexual needs met.

Masturbation, as you can imagine, is a massively taboo subject in the church. It's not talked about, but that doesn't mean it doesn't exist. On the contrary, David Clarke, who counsels many Christian couples, says it's prevalent.

> Ideally, you save yourselves for when you can be together. But there are times when you are thinking about your wife that masturbation can be appropriate and all right. That can be the

exception. What we want is sexual intimacy every three or four days. Fluids and semen build up and they need to go somewhere. Women are horrified by it because they think it's so dirty and nasty, but it doesn't have to be. Unfortunately if masturbation becomes a real habit, sooner or later Satan is going to drag you away from thinking about your wife to thinking about someone else. He will not miss that chance so we don't want to go there.[19]

You may be thinking, *My husband doesn't struggle with masturbation or sexual temptation. He's the exception.* Dr. Clarke responds,

If you say you don't struggle with temptation sexually as a man, you are a liar. Or you are the most excellent Christian we have ever produced. But I don't believe that. I go with the liar. Look at the culture—sexual temptation is everywhere. He's forced to deal with it, which makes your sexual relationship all the more important. The sexual relationship is by God's design the way we fight temptation. So if we don't have a healthy sex life, the man is doomed. He has to deal with it himself, that's true. But man alive, help us out.[20]

From Prude to Shrewd

Your husband doesn't dream of nice in the bedroom. He wants naughty. Clarke says with a laugh, "You want someone who's going to attack you in a leotard if you could have it."[21]

David Frisbie says growing up in a church with a loving family is pretty much how anyone would want his or her daughter to grow up. Except that some of those women have been programmed to believe sex is dirty and evil, and they find it difficult to flip the switch once married. Girls save themselves for marriage, and then after marriage, they keep saving themselves.

She's grown up sheltered from and afraid of sexuality. She is afraid to express sexuality because at a subconscious level, that's just evil in her brain. It's hard to overcome that barrier, but it is well worth doing. God is the creator and inventor of sex. God did not have to make it fun. This was optional on God's part. He made it a delightful thing. I don't really want to change the way these women grow up away from the culture, but we have to get over this hurdle that sex is evil and doing sexual things is evil.[22]

As wives, we have the choice between being a prude or being shrewd. The prude says, "Men are such animals. All they want is sex, sex, sex." Shrewd says, "My husband is being bombarded by sexual temptation every day, and so am I. Sex is important to my marriage so I better get with the program."

Bill and Pam Farrel have this advice in their book *Red-Hot Monogamy*:

> In your mind's eye, picture your body. What would you like your red-hot lover to do as he:
>
> > Touches your head?
> >
> > Shoulders?
> >
> > Arms?
> >
> > Hands and fingers?
> >
> > Chest/breasts?
> >
> > Stomach, hips?
> >
> > Thighs?
> >
> > Legs?
> >
> > Feet and toes?…
>
> What makes you breathe harder? Faster? What makes your heart race? What makes your mind leave today's responsibilities and enter that place of ecstasy?…No human has the ability to read a mind, so there are only a few ways your spouse will know what pleases you:
>
> - Verbally tell them.
> - Show them.
> - Give nonverbal, positive responses that are very clear.
>
> In an area as vital to marital wellness as sexual intimacy, why make it a guessing game? Make a commitment to learn to express your desires.[23]

Lessons from the Adulterous Woman

In Proverbs 7, Solomon tells the story of a young man who was ruined by an adulterous woman. You obviously don't want to become an adulterous woman, but you do want to have a love affair with your spouse. Watch what this woman does to entice the young man. The tactics she used for destruction can be used by you to save your spouse from extramarital affairs and temptations.

She notices (v. 7): "I saw among the simple, I noticed among the young men, a youth who had no sense." This woman was watching for someone to lure. She noticed him. When was the last time you consciously noticed your husband? It's easy to grow accustomed to your husband's presence as if he were wallpaper in your life. When he comes home tomorrow, really look at him the way you used to when you were dating. Notice how handsome he is. Remember how blessed you are to have him.

She initiates (v. 10): "Then out came a woman to meet him." The young man didn't have to go looking for her. She found him. When was the last time you initiated romance and lovemaking with your husband? As one husband said, "We don't always want to be the first person to start sex."

She's sexy (v. 10, 13): "Dressed like a prostitute...she took hold of him and kissed him." This adulterous woman was flaunting her assets. One commentary says perhaps she was painted as Jezebel and went with her neck and breasts bare. Whether this is the case or not, it's clear that whatever she's wearing (or not wearing) is provocative. A Christian woman has no business dressing this way in public, but in the bedroom, anything goes.

She desires him (v. 15): "I looked for you and have found you!" This man cannot deny her company when he feels so complimented. A man wants to be wanted. Your husband is no different.

She talks sweetly to him (v. 18, 21): "Come, let's drink deeply of love till morning...she seduced him with her smooth talk." Her words about her perfumed bed excite him. Her assurance that her husband is not home calms his fears. Use words with your husband to excite him and assure him of your love.

For this young man, his one-night stand ends in complete ruin. It says he was "like an ox going to the slaughter" (v. 22). But wow, when *you* love your husband madly and passionately, you're rescuing him and yourself from the destruction of that slaughterhouse.

Notice Today:

Do you acknowledge and recognize the sexual pressures and temptations your husband faces, or do you discount them?

Nurture Today:

What is one thing you can do to be more sensually alluring to your husband when you next make love? Look at the tactics used by the adulterous woman from Proverbs 7 for ideas.

Day 18

Process Not Perfection

The wife's body does not belong only to her. It also belongs to her husband. In the same way, the husband's body does not belong only to him. It also belongs to his wife.

1 CORINTHIANS 7:4 (NIRV)

A few years ago, I read about a seven-day sex challenge at a church in Dallas. In an effort to encourage intimacy in marriage, the pastor challenged the married couples in his congregation to make love every day for seven days. I decided to give it a try. James and I had sex on Saturday, Sunday, Monday, and Tuesday. By Wednesday, I just wanted to go to bed. But I had only three more days to complete my task, and I love checking off those "done" boxes in my life. James had not said anything about this experiment in romance, so I wondered if he had even noticed.

Finally I had to say something. "I've been doing a seven-day sex challenge. Did you know?" He laughed and said he didn't know. He thought it was the new normal. Then it was my turn to laugh.

Each spouse brings different expectations to the marriage bed. Some weeks, you have great times of connection. Other weeks, bare minimum maintenance seems impossible. Your husband may be deployed for months at a time. Getting on the same page sexually can be frustrating. But here's what you've got to keep in mind: You are not going for *perfection*. You want to be in the *process* of growing more intimate with your husband each year.

When Expectations Differ

Think about this last week. How many times have you and your husband been intimate? What was the quality of the sex? Cliff Penner says frequency has to get worked out between a husband and wife.

> There's not a one-size-fits-all solution. But we have generally said the married life seems to work out best if couples have sex one to two times a week. When couples come to us, they're not usually that far apart. The wife usually wants it one to two times, and the husband wants it two to three times per week.[24]

I remember a time when I could tell James was upset at me, but I didn't know why. I asked if I had done something wrong toward him. He was sad because I wasn't acting like I truly desired him sexually. He was hurt because my nightstand is stocked with "improve your sex life" books, but I didn't seem to be applying what I was learning. I was hurt because I was trying to get with the program but apparently not hard enough.

Maybe you've experienced the clash of different expectations with your spouse too. After my talk with James, I wrote in my journal that my heart needed changing. I asked God to help me develop a stronger physical desire for my husband. James told me later that he wanted to improve on his tenderness toward me with kind words, date nights, and more affection. Conversations about sex can be difficult, but they are vital to the health of the marriage. When you and your husband can talk freely about sex without the fear of being belittled or shut down, you will undoubtedly grow closer to each other.

When You Don't Look Like a Model

I had three babies and two miscarriages within six years in my thirties. I know what it's like to feel squishy in the middle and unsexy. Even with all those babies, my breasts didn't grow one iota. I walked into a bra store and asked where the "nearly A" section was. The saleslady informed me they didn't carry bras in a size so small, but I could look through the teen bras in the back of the store. Ouch.

In our visual culture, it's easy to believe the false idea that you must look like a model with an hourglass shape to be sexy. If you don't fit the bill, make sure to stay under the covers or make the room pitch-black before undressing. In their excellent book *Intimate Issues*, Linda Dillow and Lorraine Pintus have a chapter titled, "Where Can I Go to Buy a New Body?" If you're alive, you can relate.

The standard is "Thou shalt not age," but we will age. The standard is "Thou shalt be thin," but we will gain weight. As long as we continue to listen to the world's messages about our bodies, we will never be satisfied with how we look. Let's face it. There are three billion women in the world who don't look like the supermodels and only seven who do. Instead of listening to the world's message, we need to listen to what God says. God's message is: "Rejoice in the body I gave you. Use it to honor Me and please your husband."[25]

Life for you and your husband gets sweeter when you learn how to be comfortable in your own skin both inside and outside the bedroom. Tim Hawkins says, "It's unattractive when there's a lack of confidence. It gets kind of boring when women constantly harp and feel like they are focusing on their weight. A man likes a confident woman."[26]

That doesn't mean you give up on losing those twenty pounds or getting that makeup consultation. It simply means you don't demand perfection from yourself, and you understand becoming a more sensuous woman is a process. Be confident in who you are today.

Finding Art in Intimacy

In her book *Found Art*, my friend Leeana Tankersley writes about the brooding poetry she cranked out as a teenager and college student. But when she reached graduate school, she compared her work to others and found herself paralyzed.

> The voice of shame outfoxed me again, reminding me that if I couldn't create something perfect, I'd better not create anything at all…For five years, I didn't write a single poem. Not even a birthday limerick. What was the point? I couldn't well construct the epic archetypes and subversive activism my classmates managed to infuse into their masterpieces. Anything less would be pure drivel, I was convinced, and I lost the bit of truth that had been with me since junior high: art for art's sake.
>
> Perfectionism is the archnemesis of creativity. Shame, too. The big-me poet of yesterday, the fledgling artist who flung her soul headlong into expression, clammed up. That beautiful unapologetic voice became suddenly self-conscious, and I silenced a profoundly important piece of me.[27]

Now look at those words in the context of intimacy. Perhaps you have felt shameful or less than perfect in the bedroom. You've compared yourself to those annoying Victoria's Secret models. If you can't be like a sex symbol from a movie, what's the point? Perfectionism is your enemy. Don't let it silence your soul.

Bob Meissner, a pastor who has counseled many couples and is married to fiction author Susan Meissner, says, "A man wants to please his wife, to make her feel safe and loved in every way. The bedroom is a place where he can express that love."[28] Notice he didn't say the bedroom was a place to look for perfection. Instead it's a place to express love.

Who knows? When you approach it that way, you might be trying out that seven-day sex challenge this week.

Notice Today:

Do you think your husband wants to express his love in the bedroom? Have you encouraged him to take that opportunity lately?

Nurture Today:

Make a conscious effort to silence the critics in your mind that say your body isn't beautiful. View sex this week as an expression of love, not as a beauty pageant or the topic of a *Cosmopolitan* article.

Day 19

Snuggle Power

Let him kiss me with the kisses of his mouth—
for your love is more delightful than wine.

Song of Songs 1:2

James grew up camping. My family's idea of camping was visiting someone in an RV and then going back to the hotel for the night. I've come a long way since my first camping trip with James where I cried for about half the trip. James has come a long way too. The last time we went to Kings Canyon National Park in California, we stayed in a warm cabin.

On the car ride up, James asked what he could do better as a husband. Now this is a question every wife enjoys hearing. I gave him this list:

1. Go out to dinner more often.

2. Provide a little more mad money.

3. Talk to me nicer.

4. Give me massages.

Throughout our vacation, James repeated this list back to me to make sure he got it straight. He rubbed my head and neck while *he* was driving. It all definitely proved he had been listening. By the time we arrived at the cabin and got the kids asleep, it was easy to kiss and gaze into each other's eyes like star-crossed lovers. Snuggle power had been activated.

Plug in the Crock-Pot

Dr. Kevin Leman's book *Sex Begins in the Kitchen* says it well. A mother returns to her home late at night after volunteering at church. She dreads the sink full of dishes waiting for her.

> She stops dead in her tracks as she sees a beautiful, sparkling-clean kitchen. And let me tell you: the guy may have a bald spot on the back of his head, his stomach may hang over his belt—just a little—and he may give the appearance that he's trying hard to grow a second chin. But the old fellow has never looked more desirable to his wife than he does right now. And that's what I mean when I tell you that sex begins in the kitchen.[29]

You've heard the saying that men are like microwaves and women are like Crock-Pots. Words of kindness can turn on the Crock-Pot. Cleaning kitchens and other acts of service keep that Crock-Pot humming along. Husbands can activate the "snuggle power" in their wives through tender words, affection, and acts of service.

Kiss the Microwave

Even though a man can heat up in no time, chances are your husband likes physical affection and flirting more than you think. After we had kids, I was afraid to kiss James because we all know that kissing leads to sex, right? So if you don't have time for sex, don't kiss your mate.

David Clarke's book *Kiss Me Like You Mean It* gives a kissing test. There's the pathetic little peck kiss, the poofy-lip kiss (while standing far apart, the couple leans in to kiss one another), the sound-effect kiss from across the room, and the dreaded kiss on the check.[30] Do any of these describe a main staple in your kissing diet?

Movies and romance novels would lead us to believe that kissing happens spontaneously, a product of raw desire. After years of marriage and a few kids, you find that kissing takes effort and is actually more intentional than emotional. Dr. Clarke says,

> Kissing is ongoing work. It's not like the movies where you have all the chemistry. That's always true early in the relationship, but the movies don't take us all the way through. Culture says, "You can't have it decade after decade. Don't expect that. You're going to get divorced and move on and find someone else." Well that's not what God says. You've got to keep those romantic behaviors going. The make-out sessions are very important during the

week. It's leading up to the main event, but that may be a day or two away. All that anticipation is part of the deal. It's wonderful.[31]

After talking with Dr. Clarke, I thought to myself, *Make-out sessions?* Hmm, when was the last time James and I had one of those? When you have young children (ours are two, five, and seven), the make-out sessions are often scrapped for family cuddle times. I realize now that a husband and wife need to have private cuddle times too. A healthy dose of kissing does a lot to boost a marriage. So much so that Cliff and Joyce Penner recommend five to thirty seconds of passionate kissing every day. Joyce says,

> If there was one key to leave you with, it would be to kiss passionately. When he knows I'm going to kiss passionately every day, but it has nothing to do with whether I want sex tonight— it has to do with "I love you" and it feels so good—it's going to keep my pilot light on so I can get more turned-on on a regular basis. We love kissing.[32]

Everyday Snuggle Power

Here are a few things you can do today to activate snuggle power in your marriage:

Hold hands. Whenever you're walking together, get into the habit of holding hands. If you're carrying things or kids this may not be practical. But whenever you can, grab his hand as you walk or when you're sitting next to each other.

Dr. Clarke says you can tell who the married couples are at the beach because they're the ones who aren't holding hands. He wants to tell them, "If you're not going to hold hands, get off the beach. Do you know how valuable this beachfront real estate is? There are couples waiting to walk on the beach who want to hold hands."

Steal a kiss. I remember at church one day, James pulled me into an empty classroom and kissed me. It took only thirty seconds but made quite an impression. Look for opportunities to steal a kiss: in the garage before he leaves, in the kitchen when the kids are upstairs, or the backyard when he's doing chores.

Massage his neck, shoulders, hands, or feet. After a stressful day at work, massages are heavenly. Take two minutes and rub your husband's neck and shoulders after dinner. James also loves foot rubs at the end of the day, although I think they tickle.

Touch him. Snuggle up next to him while watching TV or a movie. Rest your hand on his shoulder. Grab him from behind and give him a great big bear hug. Rub his back when he's seated next to you.

Text him. Send him a message saying you miss him or send a funny private joke between the two of you. Text him when something happens during the day that reminds you of him. Just make sure it's something good. Keep the flirtations going throughout the day.

Develop a love code. Tim Hawkins's friend was having a sex talk with his thirteen-year-old daughter, and she said, "That's what you're doing when the doors are locked? I thought you were talking about Christmas presents." So now Tim will tell his wife, Heather, "Honey, we need to go talk about Christmas presents."[33]

Write him a love letter. You can't spray perfume on a phone or kiss an email with lipstick. The good old-fashioned love letter is never out of style. Here's an old love letter I found from my courting days with James in 1998:

> Dearest James,
>
> I'm absolutely crazy about you...Thank you for being such a wonderful friend to love. Thanks for the lovely flowers, the roses are beautiful. Every time I look at them, they look prettier and prettier. You are the sweetest and my dream come true. I thank God for a love like ours, a love that comes around once in a lifetime.
>
> Love,
> Ar

Now it's time for you to find your husband and give him a long, passionate kiss. Snuggle power to the rescue.

Notice Today:

Describe how you physically touched each other when you were dating.

Nurture Today:

Tell your husband about this chapter and kiss for five to thirty seconds each day for the rest of this month. If your husband isn't used to this snuggle power, he won't know what's come over you. But he probably will like it.

Guide 4

Domestic Tranquillity

Respect

Eros

Attraction
Your husband needs to be attracted to you.

Mutual Activities

Chocolate Anyone?

*So whether you eat or drink or whatever you
do, do it all for the glory of God.*

1 CORINTHIANS 10:31

At church on Mother's Day, mothers were given a heart-shaped magnet that read, "Lord, you have my heart." Sometime later, I glanced at that magnet as I opened the fridge. I had scrounged through my kids' leftover Easter chocolates and was pouring a glass of milk. Looking at the magnet, I said to the Lord, *You may have my heart, but I would like to keep my stomach.*

When it comes to chocolate, most women get protective and defensive. Of course we all know that too much of a good thing turns into a bad thing on our hips, thighs, and other places. Weight can easily become an issue in your marriage, but your husband is probably too smart to say anything about it.

In his book *His Needs, Her Needs,* Willard Harley describes your husband's fundamental need for an attractive spouse. This is not politically correct, but it's dead-on accurate.

> By calling for a wife to be attractive, I mean she should take pains to look something like the woman her husband married. After all, that was the woman he fell in love with, not a movie star or some other fantasy. Does this mean a woman must stay eternally young? Of course not, but getting older provides no excuse for letting weight creep up and up, not fixing your hair, and dressing like a bag lady.[1]

Did you notice the word *pains*? Staying attractive through the years isn't easy. It takes effort to look like you did on the day you were married. When you were dating, your husband found your body type attractive. Your figure, face, and fashion sense caught his eye. He was hooked on your looks. Now that you're married, he still wants to be hooked on your looks. That's why it so disheartening to a man when a wife lets herself go. Does that sound harsh?

This illustration may help a bit. My friend Edie shared with our Sunday school class how she'd rather go to work in her pajamas. Why not be productive *and* comfortable at the same time? But of course, every day she gets dressed, puts on makeup, and styles her hair. Why? So she can be approachable to others. Out of consideration for her coworkers, she spends time to make herself attractive. Whether we like it or not, our outward appearance does affect others.

When you take time and effort to be attractive for your spouse, what do you think that communicates to him? *I want you to approach me. I care about you. You're still the one for me.* If you can find a meaningful reason to be attractive and healthy, you have a recipe for true success.

Keeping the Pounds at Bay

Keeping weight off is an up-at-dawn, down-at-dusk siege against all the comfort foods that surround us. Waking up in the morning or heading to the gym after work isn't for the faint of heart. You've got to have the "why" firmly in place before you can start making strides in your health. You also want to be balanced, not obsessing over your weight all the time. Here are a few tips to get you moving in the right direction:[2]

Hold off on buying clothes in a size bigger. When your pants are getting tight, it's not time to go shopping. It's time to cut calories and join a gym. Don't simply lie down and let inertia take its toll. Get up and fight. Your friends may tell you weight gain is inevitable. Why *can't* you be the exception? If you give in and start buying a few new pieces in a bigger size, before you know it, your whole wardrobe will be in that bigger size. Then in a few years, this process will repeat itself. Make up your mind to hold the line—the waistline that is.

Keep a food journal. You may be completely unaware of what's going into your mouth every day. A food journal will help you assess your current eating habits, identify your weak areas, reveal your calorie intake, and hold you accountable to health goals. You can write it down on paper or use the latest app on your phone.

Be a picky eater. Choose nutrient-dense foods. Make smart swaps like skim milk instead of whole milk and unsweetened applesauce instead of sweetened. Order baked chicken instead of fried. Get oven-baked potato wedges instead of french fries. Experiment with reducing the amount of sugar in recipes and using spices like cinnamon or nutmeg when baking. If you consistently make small healthy swaps all day long, you'll see results on the scale. Why not make it a game? As you're looking at an unhealthy food you want, ask yourself, *What can I swap for that?* Recently at a coffee date, my friend looked at a Chai tea latte drink with four hundred calories and opted for the iced coffee with zero calories. That was a smart swap.

Shop differently at the grocery store. Aisle after aisle of boxed simple carbs may be on sale, but they won't help your waistline. Instead, concentrate on the produce section, and then work your way around the edge of the store until you make a square. Shop for dairy products, chicken, fish, fruit, and vegetables. Find healthy foods you and your family can really enjoy eating.

Drink plenty of water. Water suppresses your appetite and helps your body burn stored fat. It's great for your skin and has zero calories. Plus it's free. Here are a few ideas for getting more water into your daily routine:

- Always carry a water bottle with you when you go out.

- Drink a glass of water with every meal.

- Have a glass of water on your desk when you work on the computer.

- When you're hungry between meals, drink a glass of water before having your snack.

- Keep water on your nightstand at night.

Guard your pantry. If you're trying to lose weight, you've got to get rid of the temptations in your home. Not long ago we had a guest stay with us who asked if we had anything sweet to eat besides fruit. Since I was trying to lose baby weight at the time, I could not find one piece of chocolate, one cookie, one dessert in the house. It was comical. I used to keep a stash of dark chocolate behind the Crock-Pot. When I got serious about losing weight, I threw the bag away (after eating a few). It's very simple: if you don't have junk food in the house, you won't eat it.

Make exercise part of your life. Make it your goal to exercise for thirty minutes five days a week or for one hour three days a week. Include cardiovascular workouts such as cycling, jogging, swimming, and aerobics to get your heart pumping and weight training to tone your muscles and strengthen your bones. Want to increase your chances of success in keeping your exercise resolutions? Partner with a friend or, better yet, your husband.

When I interviewed seventy-year-old pastor and author David Jeremiah, he had ridden twenty miles on a bicycle the day before. He explained, "As we grow older, all of us struggle with weight. It's constantly before us. I care about trying to stay in shape because of my wife. I had fun riding my bike, I loved doing it, but part of it is also that I don't want my wife to have to grow up with an old man."[3] What a great example of the correlation between taking care of yourself physically and showing your spouse you care.

Don't Forget to Laugh

Weight loss is an emotionally charged topic for women. When I was close to my goal weight, I sprained my ankle, which slowed me down considerably. One evening I looked in the mirror and said to James, "I'm picturing what I will look like when I'm toned."

"Me too," he said.

"Lay off, honey." I pretended to be very offended and indeed, I was a little miffed.

"No, I meant for myself," he said.

Ah, a wise man. If you can laugh along the way, it makes the journey of becoming healthier much more palatable. When your husband sees you eating smart and exercising hard, he might just take you out for a slice of chocolate cake to celebrate. Here's to keeping your husband hooked on your looks.

Notice Today:

If your husband introduced you to an acquaintance, would he be proud of the way you look?

Nurture Today:

Write down your next small step to improve your eating habits, along with the date(s) you will do it:

Write down your next small step to improve your exercise habits, along with the date(s) you will do it:

Day 21

Extreme Home Makeover

Do nothing out of selfish ambition or vain conceit.
Rather, in humility value others above yourselves.

PHILIPPIANS 2:3

A few years ago, my home was chosen to appear on Season 8 of the home-improvement show *Home Made Simple* on TLC (The Learning Channel). How funny that my episode was titled "Start Your Engines Bedroom." But unfortunately for James, it didn't have anything to do with the master bedroom or romancing a happy husband. It had everything to do with transforming the nursery into a car-themed room for our six-year-old son, Ethan. The cast and crew spent four nonstop days shooting the episode and building a race-car bed, car-themed desk, and traffic-light storage cabinet. Their total room makeover focused on Ethan's love of cars.

Like Ethan's room, could you use a makeover in your wardrobe, makeup, or hairstyle to rev it up? Now before you get excited and grab your credit card to head for the mall, I want you to focus on your husband: What does he find attractive? How can you honor his preferences in the way you look? Remember, we're trying to hook him on your looks again.

Your Clothes

Most of us don't want our husbands telling us what and what not to wear. But I've learned through the years that if I bring something home from the store and James says, "That doesn't look good on you," I should return it. Usually when he says this, I already know the item is not stunning, but it seemed good enough (or cheap enough) to buy.

Having three young kids and working from home, my main wardrobe consists of T-shirts, shorts, jeans, and sweat suits. Since James frequently sees me dressed like this, I've tried to buy flattering activewear so I feel comfy but don't look frumpy. Think "comfy not frumpy" when shopping. Invest in an attractive activewear jacket and pants that fit nicely. Say good-bye to the baggy sweats and formless gray sweatshirt.

My friend Luciana's husband likes seeing her in red. It's not her favorite color, but it does look great on her. Guess what she does? She wears red to please her husband. Is that wrong because she's denying her own sense of style? Maybe if she wore red every day and hated it, but she wears it on occasion simply because her husband likes it.

Your Hair

When I married James, I had really short hair. That's the way he fell in love with me so it must have been working, right? He always talked about how much he liked long hair and would I consider growing it out? If you look at my picture on the back of this book, you'll see I was persuaded. Hair has been the subject of many jokes and a few spats between us through the years. I do like my hair long, but I probably would have chopped it off a few times in the last ten years if it didn't matter to James.

This may sound too controlling to you, so keep in mind each couple has to decide how much sway the spouse holds in giving opinions on appearance. James came home from a trip with a full beard. He could have passed me in the airport and I would have kept walking. He shaved it a few days later, but if he hadn't, I would have been petitioning day and night for the return of my clean-shaven husband. I thought he looked ridiculous.

Your Scent

When James and I were dating, he would spray cologne (Polo Sport by Ralph Lauren) on his love notes to me. I would spray perfume (Pleasures by Estee Lauder) on his love notes. We have a box full of old love letters. After more than a dozen years, a few of those envelopes still smell good. Why not put on one of your husband's favorite perfumes? Maybe it's been a while since he smelled a certain scent that will take him back to your dating days. Or try a new scent and have a perfume-smelling date night. My friend Leeana Tankersley got these suggestions via Facebook for favorite fragrances to try:

Journey by Mary Kay

Happy by Clinique

Tea Rose by Perfumer's Workshop

Poppy by Coach

J'adore by Christian Dior

Romance by Ralph Lauren

Chance by Chanel

Michael by Michael Kors

Red by Giorgio Beverly Hills

Your Makeup

Bob Lepine likes when his wife, Mary Ann, pulls her hair away from her face and wears just a little makeup. He's not a big makeup guy. On the other hand, my James likes makeup and will tell me not to be so frugal when it comes to applying it. Every man is different. Do you know what makeup looks your husband likes? You can show him magazine pictures, ads at cosmetic counters, or examples of women you know to get an idea of his preferences.

Does this mean we have to be little puppets, asking our husbands for permission before buying lipstick, getting a haircut, or shopping for a new top? That would get complicated and ridiculous. I'm simply saying you can welcome his input about your hairstyle, makeup, and clothes instead of immediately dismissing his opinions. What does *he* know about style? Well, if you want your husband to find you attractive, apparently he knows a great deal.

Catch His Eye Again

Going back to *Home Made Simple*, one of the hosts is contractor Patrick Brown. He met his wife-to-be in the grocery store. He noticed her wearing a ring with a cross. As they talked, it was apparent she followed Christ, as did Patrick. A year later, he proposed on Valentine's Day. Patrick was attracted by her outward beauty, and her inner beauty sealed the deal. He says,

> When a wife takes care of her appearance as mine has, it communicates volumes to the husband. Dress yourself up as much as

you can, understanding that your husband is a gift to you from God. You want to present yourself to him as if you are presenting yourself to the Lord Himself. I think women more than anything need to accept the way God made them, and they need to try to be the best that God has made them.[4]

Months or years ago, the way you looked caught your husband's eye. You can catch his eye again today—let the extreme home makeover begin.

Notice Today:

What types of looks does your husband like (clothes, makeup, hair)? What are his favorite outfits on you?

Nurture Today:

On your next date, wear something you know your husband really likes. Plan your outfit with only him in mind.

Day 22

I Still Do

*"For this reason a man will leave his father
and mother and be united to his wife,
and the two will become one flesh."*

Matthew 19:5

You've heard of the movie *When Harry Met Sally*. Let me tell you the real-life story of when Lou met Sally. Like the movie, a life-changing event happened at a New Year's Eve party, but this party happened in the 1940s. Lou met Sally and thought she was easily the prettiest girl there. Too bad she was his friend's date and only a fifteen-year-old junior in high school. Lou was an eighteen-year-old high school graduate. A few years later, Lou ran into Sally again on the campus of the University of Washington. He looked her up in the yearbook and asked her on a date. By then, his friend had lost interest and Lou thought his friend "did not appreciate quality when he saw it." [5]

Attracted by her inner beauty and fun nature, Lou began dating Sally, though they both continued to date others. Then Lou left school to earn good money at an engineering job. When he returned two years later in 1950, he was surprised to find Sally still single. He realized he'd better do something about that before someone else discovered what a jewel she was. They married in June of 1953.

Lou's favorite trip was their one-month-long honeymoon driving across Canada in their 1951 Ford filled with all their worldly possessions. They drove east toward Lou's new job in Baltimore. To save money, they camped in a pup tent for most of those days, but that didn't bother the honeymooners. They bought a five-pound block of frozen hamburger, which served as the ice for their ice chest. Sally shaved off the thawed-out layer of hamburger each day and cooked meat loaf in a wood-fired camp-ground oven.

Through the decades, Lou and Sally have had many adventures scuba diving, snorkeling, traveling in their RV, skiing, swimming, and more. You name it and they've probably done it. If you spend any amount of time with them, one thing is clear. They still do believe the wedding vows they spoke in 1953.

From Dairy Queen to James's Queen

Although I loved my college experience at Biola University, I man-aged to graduate without that coveted MRS degree. Four years later, I was in graduate school when a certain young man flipped my hamburger at a student orientation. A few weeks later, I met that same handsome young man named James in a van load of students headed for a nursing home. It was a Friday night, and we were going to sing for the residents and visit with them. When James shared a Bible study with the residents, half might have been sleeping, but I was wide awake praying, *Oh Lord, I want to marry that man.*

We became good friends, and I interpreted every invitation to Dairy Queen for ice cream blizzards to use his "buy one get one free" coupon as a sure sign of progress. But he just wanted to be friends. After a year and a half, I *finally* got the message. About the same time I gave up, James was opening his eyes to the possibility of love.

He was planning to take me to his usual place—Dairy Queen—but thankfully the university librarian suggested something a little more appropriate for the occasion. At Outback Steakhouse, James pulled out two roses—a yellow one for friendship and a red one for love. He said we had been friends and that he would like to court me. That was the best dessert at Outback I've ever had.

After that dessert date, we were inseparable. We took a road trip to New York City to visit his family for a few days. My mom asked, "What if you don't get along and you're trapped with him for a few days?" I told her she had nothing to worry about.

I've been happily trapped with James ever since.

You have a love story about how you and your husband got "trapped" together. Tim Hawkins was friends with his wife, Heather, for two years before he proposed in the parking lot of her apartment complex. He laughs about kneeling in an oil stain to propose, then having a wedding reception with Kool-Aid, Ritz crackers, and cheese squares.

Isn't it fun to keep the stories of your early years with your spouse close to heart? You've got to remember through the good times and bad that you "didn't marry Hitler's distant cousin" as Emerson Eggerichs said on a Focus on the Family webcast.[6]

The Polar Bear Club

When we were first married, James thought I'd be wearing a sexy little nightgown to bed every night. I guess that's why my sleep shirt had become a bone of contention. Bought years ago, it's navy blue with three-quarter sleeves and says "Polar Bear Club" on the front. It has an athletic feel to it with the number 54 on the front. Don't guys like sports? And a polar bear's got to be more fierce than, let's say, a koala bear, right? So I don't really get what the problem is with wearing a comfortable T-shirt to bed.

The "Polar Bear Club" was a frosty and rude awakening for James. I quickly rebutted, "When it's cold at night, you don't come to bed in a pair of boxers. Why should I freeze in a little negligee?" That seemed to end the discussion. So I've been sporting my "Polar Bear Club" favorite T-shirt and pajama bottoms to bed for years.

James has a group of guy friends from college that he meets with every few years from all over the country. James shared his "Polar Bear Club" dilemma with the guys. "How can I get rid of this nasty T-shirt?" I think the way he described it to his buddies made them think I went to bed every night in a black burka.

Bryant, who had been James's chaplain in college, had faced a similar problem with his wife. So he—get this—had a fireplace installed in their room. Then he threw out all her pajamas and took her shopping to Victoria's Secret, where they both picked out her new bedtime wardrobe. She did get to pick cute comfy pajamas that they both found attractive.

You need some deep pockets to pull off a fireplace and shopping spree, but it reminds me of the time James bought me a bikini for eighty dollars. Knowing James's frugal nature, my dad said, "I can't believe you spent that much money for that." James replied, "Wouldn't you spend that much money to see your wife in that?" Discussion ended.

So for Mother's Day, guess what James bought me? Packages mailed from Victoria's Secret started pouring in. To my relief, they were tank tops and shorts I could be comfy in. One was a long T-shirt that would give me the same warmth that my beloved "Polar Bear Club" shirt gave. And I already had matching gray leggings to go with it, to which James responded, "No. I didn't buy the pajama top for you to put pants underneath. That defeats the whole purpose. Put *that* in your book."

I haven't given my beloved shirt to Goodwill yet, but I haven't worn it again either. I still do want my husband to find me attractive in bed even fifty years from now. Wonder what Victoria's Secret will be selling then?

Notice Today:

How did you and your husband meet? Do you still want to win his heart over like you did then? Take out your wedding album and relive a few moments with your husband.

Nurture Today:

Ask your husband what he likes you to wear to bed. Maybe you have a "Polar Bear Club" shirt that needs to be retired too.

Day 23

Happy Wife, Happy Life

The fruit of the Spirit is love, joy, peace…

GALATIANS 5:22

When Ethan was about four, I enlisted him to do a video promo for a women's retreat. I had him at a sink full of dishes saying, "At the retreat, there will be no dishes." Then he was jumping up and down on his bed saying, "You can stay up as long as you want." Finally, he was lying on a couch, kicking back with his hands behind his head, saying smugly, "Happy wife, happy life."

And all the husbands say "Amen." When a wife is happy or unhappy, everyone in the household knows. James says if he had to boil down this book to one principle, it would be *a husband wants an attractive spouse who is smiling from ear to ear.*

Financial speaker and author Scott Palmer echoes James's sentiment:

> I want to know that my wife is happy. If she's whining or miserable or tired, that's a huge buzzkill. I think many people have unhappy marriages because the wife is unhappy. The "I love yous" and support are important, but I just need to hear my wife say, "Hey, I'm having a great time." Bethany tells me all the time, "I love our life together." That's all I need. I just need to know that she's happy.[7]

This is sounding pretty good, right? If your husband wants a happy wife, isn't that what you want too? You want to be happy, so why is it so difficult sometimes?

I was in a department store with my daughter Noelle, who was eighteen months old at the time. She was giggling and happy. The tired-looking saleslady bent down and told Noelle, "Yeah, that's because you're riding around in a stroller. Just wait until you have a job and have to work all day. We'll see if you're smiling then."

I think if I pushed that lady around in a stroller all day, she would still find something else to complain about. Happiness isn't so much about circumstances. It's about something far deeper.

Happiness from Above

When we follow the instructions to wives laid out in the Bible, regardless of how we feel, regardless of the outcome, we will be blessed. Obedience to God's Word brings joy. Solomon wrote in Ecclesiastes 2:26, "To the person who pleases him, God gives wisdom, knowledge and *happiness*."

Since this is the case, how can we as wives please God in our marriages? The apostle Peter gives us some specific instruction on ways we can do this.

"Wives, in the same way submit yourselves to your own husbands" (1 Peter 3:1). Give your husband loving and reverent respect, yielding to his authority as the leader in the home.

"So that, if any of them do not believe the word, they may be won over without words by the behavior of their wives when they see the purity and reverence of your lives" (3:1-2). There's nothing like kindness and devotion expressed through actions to soften the heart of a husband, believing or unbelieving.

"Your beauty should not come from outward adornment...Rather, it should be that of your inner self, the unfading beauty of a gentle and quiet spirit" (vv. 3-4). Keep in mind many of the wives Peter was writing to were married to pagan, harsh husbands that would make your man look like a puppy dog.

Matthew Henry's commentary says it this way: "Christians ought to do their duty to one another, not out of fear, nor from force, but from a willing mind, and in obedience to the command of God. Wives should be in subjection to their churlish husbands, not from dread and amazement, but from a desire to do well and to please God."[8]

Continuing in 1 Peter 3, the following instructions are for all of us, not just husbands and wives.

> Finally, all of you, be like-minded, be sympathetic, love one
> another, be compassionate and humble. Do not repay evil with

evil or insult with insult. On the contrary, repay evil with blessing, because to this you were called so that you may inherit a
blessing. For,

> "Whoever would love life
>   and see good days
> must keep their tongue from evil
>   and their lips from deceitful speech.
> They must turn from evil and do good;
>   they must seek peace and pursue it.
> For the eyes of the Lord are on the righteous
>   and his ears are attentive to their prayer,
> but the face of the Lord is against those who do evil."
>   (1 Peter 3:8-12)

This is the prescription given for a happy life in an unhappy world.
When you are a team player, seeking peace and keeping your tongue from
evil, you will be happy. The peace of Christ will reign in your life. Happiness comes when you get on the same page as God.

In her book *When a Woman Inspires Her Husband*, Cindi McMenamin
writes,

> Are you willing to trust God that as you please Him by serving
> your husband He will make it worth your while? Look at it this
> way: If you are laying down yourself so you can please someone
> else (God and your husband), God is not going to make you mis-
> erable in return. Trust Him. Trust the process.[9]

Blessed Not Stressed

Marriage counselor David Frisbie has heard it all. He thanks God for
a wife who obeys the Word of God and exudes happiness in their home.

> I deal with negative energy all day, every day. Always have, prob-
> ably always will. I really think it's why God created me. I don't
> resent it or regret it. But when I am done with work, I am not
> ready to take on more negative energy. I'm just not. For my wife,
> Lisa, to be this wellspring of positive, refreshing encouragement
> is just profound. I would unravel quickly if I lived in a stressed
> home. When I go home from stress all day, I need to be in the
> least stressed environment I can possibly be in. And she has
> always made it that, no matter what the circumstance.[10]

You know what the good news is? You can choose to be happy even if you have little practical experience with smiling lately. You don't have to wait for your husband to obey God's Word about marriage before you begin. You can obey God's commands and trust *Him* to pour joy into you.

A story called "Wife's Imaginary List" illustrates one way we can nurture our attitude as a happy wife:

> At her Golden Wedding celebration, my grandmother told guests the secret of her happy marriage: "On my wedding day, I decided to make a list of ten of my husband's faults which, for the sake of our marriage, I would overlook." As the guests were leaving, a young matron whose marriage had recently been in difficult straights asked my grandmother what some of the faults were that she had seen fit to overlook. Grandmother said, "To tell you the truth, my dear, I never did get around to listing them. But whenever my husband did something that made me hopping mad, I would say to myself, 'Lucky for him that's one of the ten.'"[11]

That sounds like a wise list to have in your back pocket. *Happy wife, happy life.*

Notice Today:

When you are unhappy, how does that affect your husband?

Nurture Today:

The next time your husband does something that irritates you, make it one of the things on your list of faults to overlook.

Day 24

No Drama Divas Here

Fools give full vent to their rage,
but the wise bring calm in the end.

PROVERBS 29:11

Here's a funny experiment you can try at home. Go into the bathroom after you've talked to your husband about something that has you really excited or upset. Pretend you're still talking to your husband and reenact a few lines from the conversation while looking at yourself in the mirror. Pay attention to your facial expressions, gestures, and voice. Are you talking really fast or looking like you're trying to land a 747?

Most men aren't used to this kind of emotion in conversation. Think about the interactions with people your husband has most of the day. Nobody else in their world probably talks like you, and that's okay. But keep in mind that drama can be overdone, leaving a husband to write his wife off as a "drama babe."

I asked Bob Lepine, with his experience hosting *Family Life Today* on the radio, about the effect of too much needless drama on a husband.

> The amount of passion a woman will express about a viewpoint or about what she's feeling is often disproportionate to what's really going on inside of her. He's thinking this is a huge deal, when it's not a huge deal. It's just how she communicates. She's a drama queen. Everything's a huge deal, right? So it puts him at a disadvantage. How does he know when something really is a huge deal when everything is a huge deal?
>
> The wife needs to learn how to express her emotions and passions in such a way that she's honestly reflecting how important

something is. And that means she has to be self-aware and recal-
ibrate. She can come around and say, 'I made a bigger deal of that
than I needed to.' That helps the husband.[12] [13]

You don't need a scientific study to conclude that men find women baf-
fling. Sometimes, no matter how hard he tries, your husband just doesn't
get you. I love the story Tim Hawkins shared about his wife, Heather. They
were at a restaurant with their menus open and Tim asked her, "What do
you want?" She replied, "I want you to want to know what I want." This
totally blew Tim's mind. He's thinking, *I just asked you what you want. Am
I in a parallel universe?*

Another day, Tim and Heather were in the grocery store, and Heather
said, "I want you to want to go to the grocery store with me." Again,
Tim's confused because isn't he standing in the grocery store with his wife
already? He says, "I don't know what to say to that. I'm generally perplexed.
I need another eighteen years to figure you out."[13]

Then Came Zane

What if you are not a drama babe and you're trying your best to communicate succinctly, but life has thrown you some dramatic twists and
turns? John Fuller, host of *Focus on the Family,* and his wife, Dena, know a
thing or two about having their world turned upside down. They have six
children. Enough said, right? With five biological children, they adopted
their sixth child from Russia. John remembers,

> We were feeling pretty comfortable in our parenting and in the
> family routines. Our youngest was three, and she was out of
> diapers. We kind of foolishly and naively thought, *We have five,
> what's one more?* In His humorous way, God said, "I'll tell you
> what one more is." And He rocked our world. Number one, that
> whole adoption journey. That paper pregnancy is way longer
> than a regular pregnancy and way more expensive. Finally, we
> brought our little guy home when he was nine months old.[14]

One year after bringing him home and working through major attach-
ment issues, John and Dena knew something else was wrong with their
new son Zane. The diagnosis of autism shook them to the core. As a
stay-home mom, Dena has worked endlessly to give her other five kids a

semblance of normal while taking Zane to speech therapy, occupational therapy, counseling, group social skills classes, and more. Zane is now eight and has made tremendous progress. John says,

> It's been all hands on deck to help Zane get the tools he needs to make it in this world, to function. It has been frankly draining and all-consuming. You pray a lot. We've gone to the Lord and said, "We can't do this. Here we are, empower us, in our weakness please be strong." The lessons we've learned are absolutely worth it. I think the Lord's used Zane to tenderize our hearts and given us a great awareness of people who have much harder circumstances than this.[15]

I asked John what Dena has done as a wife to bless him during this difficult and dramatic season of life. How can you be attractive as a wife when you're under so much physical and emotional stress? Here's what I learned from John's comments:

Pray for your husband. Dena gets up early in the morning and has her time alone with God, praying and reading the Bible. She desperately hungers and thirsts after God.

"I want to tell you that makes such a difference," John says. "Who knows how much prayer has been answered, but I know it's a lot. It's crucial for women to understand when you quietly pray behind the scenes, that affects your attitude, your heart, the whole tenor of the home, and your guy's going to appreciate that deeply. I know I do."

Recognize he's not the enemy. Dena realizes they've got to work together as a team to raise an autistic child and five others. When John gets home from work, Dena pulls him into family responsibilities, relies on him, and expresses gratitude. "I'm her partner, her friend, her colaborer in this," John says. "We don't want to lose our marriage over a challenging situation like this."

Communicate clearly. John has learned to say, "What is it you need here?" Dena has learned to paraphrase and set expectations for the conversation so she's not always venting and dumping. "She's gone out and gotten friends that can listen well. I can't provide it all for her, so I thank God for friends she goes walking with once a week to pray with and talk about things. That takes effort on her part, but that helps me because the burden to be all things to my dear wife is just something I can't shoulder."

Working at a place like Focus on the Family, John and Dena are very aware that far too many good Christian people just don't make it in their marriages. Too many families are fractured. John says thoughtfully that it might be in God's grace that He gave them an "all hands on deck" child to keep Dena and him connected and to keep them dependent on Him.

Isn't that a refreshing way to look at drama in your life?

Flat Daddy

Deployment is a traumatic time for many husbands, wives, and children. When James's grad-school buddy, Doug, spent thirteen months in Baghdad as an army chaplain, his wife, Ally, did something wonderfully dramatic for Doug and their three young children. She made a six-foot "Flat Daddy" out of corrugated foam board with Doug's head and body on it. Ally would take the "Flat Daddy" wherever they went—in the van with the kids, to baseball games, to school. Then she would take pictures of the kids hugging and kissing "Flat Daddy" in all those different locations and email them to Doug. By making memories with that life-sized cut-out, the family kept Doug front and center on their hearts. And Doug felt extremely touched to be a part of their everyday lives while he was gone.

When you find yourself depressed by the circumstances of life, read these stories again about the Fullers pulling together and "Flat Daddy" getting carted around town. With the Lord's help, you can turn your desperation into a heart-warming drama that strengthens your home instead of tearing it down.

Notice Today:

How does your husband respond to a drama queen (whether it's you or someone else)? Does he try to escape or disengage, or does he really enjoy the dialogue?

Nurture Today:

The next time you're tempted to be overly dramatic, hear the conversation from your husband's perspective. Try your best to convey the facts without extreme emotions that will most likely wear him out.

Day 25

Timeless Beauty

[Your beauty] should be that of your inner self,
the unfading beauty of a gentle and quiet spirit,
which is of great worth in God's sight.

1 Peter 3:4

How would you like your husband to say this about you? *I'm out of my league. Look at her picture, look at mine. It's the truth. Man, she's unbelievable. As beautiful as you might think she is on the outside, that woman is a home run on the inside.*

I think all of us want to be that kind of wife. Patrick Brown used those words to describe his wife, Denise. It's her inner beauty that's captivated him. Patrick says,

> The most important thing to me about my wife is her relationship with God. She is very close to God. I tell Denise, I know God loves everyone, but for some reason, He really likes you. She has the sensitivity on the inside of her that knows when God is saying something to her. That's what I find so beautiful about her. She is a person who knows right and wrong and wants to do right. I know that sounds very elementary, but I don't think it's as common as people want to think it is.[16]

Is your husband attracted to your character? I heard that character is who you are when no one is looking. If anyone has a chance to see what you're really made of, it's your husband. Are you showing him the timeless beauty of true character?

Closer Through Devotion

If you're looking for an older couple that still looks happy to be together, I've found several at my church. One of those couples is George and Mary. They've been married for sixty years. One of the secrets of their marital success has something to do with breakfast and the Bible.

While George was working, Mary and George would read their Bibles and pray on their own, though they always worshipped together in church and found it easy to talk about spiritual matters. When George retired over twenty years ago, they decided to have a daily time of Bible reading and prayer together after breakfast. Once they've enjoyed their breakfast and coffee, they are wide awake and ready to dive in. Mary says,

> We read one chapter aloud from the Old Testament and one from the New Testament. We go straight through the Bible. Afterwards we have prayer about whatever we want: different needs, missionaries, church, and loved ones. We worship God. It fluctuates as the Lord speaks to us. It's been meaningful and powerful in our lives. You grow as you're in God's Word. No matter how many times we've read it, it never gets old.[17]

Can you imagine spending time every day for more than twenty years praying and reading the Bible with your husband? That is a wonderful spiritual legacy. I share it to inspire you, not to make you feel like a devotional loser. Notice George and Mary started this habit after they were retired, not when they were in the height of their child-rearing and career-building years (although Mary does wonder now why they didn't start reading and praying together sooner).

Let Him Get the Plan

In most cases, the wife is more likely than her husband to walk into a Christian bookstore and buy a book for them to read and discuss together. Men don't typically get together and form book clubs. Wives tend to get frustrated when their husbands don't lead the way with devotions as a couple or family. But we must recognize that women are naturally wired to be more relational.

You don't want to guilt your man into leading the family spiritually. Beware of the tendency for women to control or manipulate the family spiritually under the guise of just trying to help. Too much help can push your man's soul into hiding. David Clarke offers this advice to the woman who wants to be more spiritually bonded to her Christian husband:

> Have a conversation and say, "This is one of the deepest needs of my heart. Would you lead us in prayer and Bible reading?" Let it sink in for a week. Leave it in his hands. You might say, "Let's touch base again in a week and see what you think." That gives a man a chance to own it. You don't want to pin him to the wall in the first conversation. "What's it going to be, buddy? I've made my case. What are you going to do?"

> Well, he's not going to do anything. Leave him alone. Most decent Christian men are not going to come back and say, "Sorry, but thanks for sharing." He knows it's the right thing to do. There are some books that can help guide the man through spiritual bonding. Give him some options of devotionals, Bible reading, and prayer and ease into it. Dialogue together and let him as the leader take the first steps.[18]

Pastor Glen Cole adds that the man is the key to establishing the spiritual foundation in the home. Women want to take that role sometimes, but it's not their position to take.

> Men are slower than women. A woman goes to a Bible study and comes home fired up and ready to take over. Men are more calculating, and sometimes ego gets in the way. Women who push the envelope create more problems. Give your man time and space to develop.[19]

In the book *When a Woman Inspires Her Husband*, Hugh McMenamin says,

> It's important that you not make your husband feel that he has to "report to you" about the status of his spirituality, or that you are doing a performance review of this area of his life. Ask him honest questions, and be willing to accept his honest answers. If your husband is more of a cognitive learner, buy him a book or CD on spiritual issues. If he tends to be more of a hands-on learner, see if there are any church projects in which he can work side-by-side with other men. In such cases, I guarantee you that more than just physical labor will take place.[20]

When you allow your husband to lead spiritually, you are showing him the unfading beauty of a gentle and quiet spirit (1 Peter 3:4). Instead of relying on your own strategies to lead the family, you are counting on God to work through your husband. Let your character speak. Through the years, your body will inevitably deteriorate, but there's good news. The inward beauty of your life is timeless.

Notice Today:

Are you spiritually intimidating to your husband? Does he ever think he's not measuring up spiritually by the way you act or say things?

Nurture Today:

Pray daily for your husband. If he is a Christian, allow him to be the spiritual leader of the home.

Day 26

Lovers' Lane to the Empty Nest

Two are better than one,
because they have a good return for their labor.
ECCLESIASTES 4:9

W hen I say Bill and Pam Farrel have a steep driveway, that's an under-statement. The Driveway of Death is more like it. Once when visit-ing, I tried to turn my car around because I knew I could not back down that driveway. All of a sudden, I heard a crunch and scraping sound. I had hit a stucco curb that was short enough for me to overlook but high enough to make a mark on my husband's car. Mortified and embarrassed, I had to ask Bill to maneuver my car so I could leave.

The journey between "I do" and the grave can be like that driveway of death for many couples. It starts off fun, but you get a few scrapes along the way. And if you don't ask for help when you need it, your car picks up speed and careens out of control.

But hold on, you're not a helpless passenger. There are things you can do to navigate safely between Lovers' Lane, the empty nest, retirement, and beyond.

The Warmth of Affection

Last Valentine's Day, James really outdid himself. He not only bought a dozen beautiful red roses; he tied them together artistically and arranged them in a vase. He bought me a jacket I wanted on eBay. Plus he cooked dinner for the whole family. I was expecting pizza bagels, but instead he served stir-fry chicken. After dinner, he announced that the kids were going to grandma's house and we were going out. I assumed dessert at a restaurant, but instead James drove to a park.

We walked to a picnic table with a view of the city. He took out two cups of vanilla ice cream and root beer—I love root beer floats. Then to my horror (I mean delight), he spread out a blanket and invited me to lie down with him. He started kissing me. I mean, come on, it was Valentine's Day. But all I could think was, *Oh no. We probably look like the kissing teenagers that nice moms and dads try to avoid with their kids.*

James noticed my hesitancy and said, "We used to kiss all the time when we were dating, and you didn't seem to mind. You weren't so self-conscious and worried. Now we're married—it should be more okay." I realize now the few passersby probably couldn't see us anyway. I needed to be a little less self-conscious and a little more affection conscious. I prayed that night, *Lord, help me to be more he centered and less me centered.*

When you keep kissing and showing affection years after the "I do," you're putting gas in the car to keep your love bug humming along.

Mark Matlock and his wife, Jade, have two teenagers. He wisely says,

> If you want your kids to properly experience affection, they need to see that displayed. If we don't hear our kids say, "Oh gross" at least once a day, we're not doing our job. I don't mean by that being inappropriate. It's kissing each other, sitting next to each other, holding hands. Mom and Dad being connected gives kids a lot of security.[21]

In four years, Mark's son will be college bound. I know many parents who pour *everything* into their high schoolers because they want to enjoy them while they still have them at home. Mark gave me a different perspective that I found very healthy for couples to consider.

> I realize I've got four more years with my kids, but that doesn't make me say, "Oh, I need to spend every moment with my kids." It makes me go invest in my relationship with Jade because in a few more years, it's going to be just her and me again, and I want to enjoy that. I want there still to be a relationship there. We want to be dreaming as a couple together and enjoying each other's presence now because we're going to the grave together.[22]

The transition to the empty nest devastates many couples. When the kids leave, what's there to keep the marriage together? We need more husbands and wives who echo Mark's sentiment of investing in each other first.

Making Special Memories Along the Way

My friend Bob is a man's man. He was hired thirty years ago by the San Diego Police Department and presently serves as a patrol sergeant and the SWAT sniper-team sergeant. Now that his kids are in college or working, he likes that he can take off for a weekend with his wife whenever they want without finding someone to watch the kids. (For those of us with kids at home, take heart—those days are coming.)

But Bob reminds parents in the trenches, "I find myself looking at families with young children and kind of miss the times when ours were young. We did all sorts of fun activities that the kids ate up, like camping in Arizona and our yearly boat trips to Lake Mead. So enjoy your little ones while you can."[23]

David Jeremiah says that every part of life has its own rewards and challenges. He married Donna in 1963, and their love has grown richer each year.

> Over the years, we just like being in each other's presence. Just the knowledge that she's there for me and I'm there for her, that's just so special. There's a security and familiarity that goes without saying a word. One of the joys of being together such a long time is the shared memories.[24]

The Jeremiahs make a point to create treasured memories along the way. Talking about an upcoming speaking trip to New Jersey, David said:

> Years ago when we were living in Fort Wayne, Indiana, we used to take vacations in Ocean City, New Jersey. We did that for twelve years straight. So I've rented a convertible, and Donna and I are going a week early. We're going to drive around all those places where we used to go. Take the ferry from Cape May to Lewes, Delaware, and walk down the boardwalk. You build all these memories, and you realize there's not another person in the whole world that shares that memory with you. You find yourself saying, "Do you remember that?" Or a special song will come on, and you'll say, "I remember that song." That's the way it's

supposed to work. The Bible says the two of you will become one. You're two people but one person really in so many respects.[25]

Those memories can be as grand as a Mediterranean cruise or as normal as a night at home playing cards.

> We like to play games with each other. Sometimes when we're home alone at night, I'll say, "Let's play Phase 10." Donna's a real competitor; she doesn't like to lose any more than I do.
>
> Once when we were playing Phase 10, our daughter Jan called us and said, "Hey, what are you guys doing?"
>
> "Oh, we're just here sitting at the table," Donna said.
>
> "Well, what are you doing?"
>
> "We're playing Phase 10."
>
> "Just you and Dad?"
>
> "Yes."
>
> People think that when you're older, you sit around and watch TV or something. And we don't. We have a lot of fun together.[26]

When you...

- continue kissing and holding hands
- focus your keenest attention on your mate and not your children
- enjoy the high points of every phase from the honeymoon to grandparenting
- make it a priority to create special memories

you will find yourself riding in a comfortable convertible from one wonderful place of life to another. You won't have to fear the Driveway of Death anymore.

Notice Today:

Are you and your husband in an easy or challenging part of the marriage journey?

Nurture Today:

What special memories have you had with your husband over the last few years? Make a "remember when" list and share it with him over dinner tonight (or later this week if tonight doesn't work).

Domestic Tranquillity

Respect

Eros

Attraction

Mutual Activities
Your husband needs to have fun with you.

Date Night

Let him lead me to the banquet hall,
and let his banner over me be love.

SONG OF SONGS 2:4

Someone once wisely said to me that date nights are less expensive than marriage counseling. When you have time to regularly connect with your spouse to have fun, you prevent the arctic chill from settling between you. You have the chance to laugh and remember what drew you to your man in the first place. You get a reprieve from the stress and responsibilities of work and parenting. You can talk about issues and deal with things before they grow out of proportion. Date nights give you something to look forward to. So if date nights are so great, are you doing them?

I know a few couples with children at home who date every week. They are the exception. Most couples I talk to stare blankly into space when I ask, "When was your last date night?" I even know couples who haven't gone on a date since their first child was born—and that was seven years ago.

James and I see each other a lot since we both work out of our home. He's a realtor and has breakfast and dinner with us most days. For a while, we weren't going on date nights. After all, when he would ask, "How was your day?" often he already knew the answer in Technicolor detail. But after reading the book *Kiss Me Like You Mean It*, we realized we needed to bring back the date night.

My parents, who always watch our kids, were out of town, so we had our first ever babysitter. I put on a little extra makeup, and we headed for a Cheesecake Factory only ten minutes away just in case baby Lucy decided she did not like having a babysitter. I actually had butterflies before going out. Perhaps it was nervousness about Lucy, but I think it was more excitement to be alone with James.

Trying to do the same things we used to when we were dating, we sat on the same side of the booth. That lasted through the entrée. By dessert, we switched spots because our necks hurt. That didn't solve the neckache, so James said, "Sit on the other side." We were back to normal seating, but it was fun to switch it up while our necks allowed.

A Date to Remember

For many years my friends Jim and Diane had a standing date with the San Diego Chargers. With season tickets in hand, they would get a babysitter, grab sandwiches at Submarina, and arrive at the game ninety minutes before kickoff to watch the players warm up. Diane, a people watcher, got her fill of entertainment. They cheered together, got ticked off together when things weren't going the Chargers' way, and loved every minute of it. It's a vivid memory they both share years later.

You may not enjoy watching football together, but you and your husband can find something else to do together that you both like. I asked my friends Andy and Teresa what they like to do on dates (you'll read about their crazy motorcycle date on Day 30):

> You name it, we like it. Movies, concerts, long walks, Starbucks, going to the grocery store or Walmart, raking leaves, bike rides. We love each other and love sharing life. We just celebrated thirty years and we both want a hundred more. Life is God's amazing present to us. It's even more rare when you find the perfect person to share it with.[1]

One memorable date I had with James was the "Great 24-Hour Date." You can't have one of these too often, but it's worth the planning if you can slip away for twenty-four hours once a year, twice a year, or even quarterly. We had a local friend who offered her condo for a getaway while she was out of town. Here's how we used our time:

> Friday, 12:00 noon—Went to hear an interesting speaker at Point Loma Nazarene College
>
> 4:30 p.m.—Shopping at TJ Maxx clothing store (this was actually James's suggestion)

5:30 p.m.—Dinner at Sammy's Woodfired Pizza

7:00 p.m.—Watched the movie *Kung Fu Panda* with some hot tea at the condo

9:30 p.m.—Massages, etcetera...

Saturday, 8:00 a.m.—Breakfast of pastries bought the day before

10:00 a.m.—Shopping at Fry's Electronics (note the equal guy/girl shopping time)

12:00 noon—Pick up the kids at Grandpa and Grandma's

I loved this date because we connected *intellectually* by discussing the speaker. We connected *physically* through sex and affectionate touching. We connected *emotionally* through all the talk time. And of course, we connected over delicious food and shopping for him and her. All this without any kids.

25 Cheap Dates Under $25

On Day 3 I told you about Bob and Jana and their special box of fifty-two date ideas for the whole year. They were kind enough to share some of their dates with us. You can try these as is or put your own creative twist on them.

1. Let's hike down Memory Lane and walk that trail we used to when we were dating.

2. Hope it's a sunny day. Let's ride our bikes around the bay (or lake, or park, or...).

3. Our room is one of the most romantic places for us to be. Let's order food to go and stay in our bedroom all night.

4. Let's take a spin to our old apartment and reminisce about our newlywed days.

5. Scavenger Hunt: We'll each think of five random things to be found at the park or shopping center. We have to take a picture of us with the item.

6. Let's take advantage of a dying American icon—the drive-in movie. We can snuggle in the back of the car.[2]

7. A night in—let's rent a movie—your choice. Guy flicks are fine. We'll start early.

8. Spring-time date: Let's go to Home Depot and have a hot-dog and choose some flowers to plant. Let's create something beautiful together.

9. You know in the commercials where the guy and girl are having so much fun washing the car together? Let's see if it's what it's all cracked up to be. Afterward, let's sit in the yard and watch our neighbors go by.

10. "What Not to Wear": each of us chooses one item from each other's closet that just has to go, then we shop to replace the item with something we'd like to see each other in. Wear the new item to dinner.

11. Let your artistic side shine. Let's paint a piece at the ceramic café.

12. Barnes and Noble Night.

13. Remember our java days? Let's find a coffeehouse we rarely frequent and talk about the past and the future.

14. Let's take a new hike in a new location.

15. Conversation questions by candlelight.

16. Groupon date: watch the offers this week. We'll try something new.

17. Let's try a ballroom dance class.

18. Let's plan and prepare a romantic dinner for two, and eat out on the patio.

19. Want to feel young again? How about a game of miniature golf?

20. A quiet night in. Let's do crackers and cheese and look at our old photo albums.

21. When is the last time we went bowling? I think you look sexy in those shoes.

22. It's time, we can't avoid it any longer: karaoke.

23. Take me out to the ball game. Let's sit in the bleacher seats for cheap. You can buy me some peanuts and Cracker Jacks.

24. Let's get on a trolley and go on a little adventure. No pre-planned agenda.

25. Let's research massage techniques and try them out on each other.

Ladies, Friday night is coming. Which date will you and your man enjoy this weekend? Remember, dating is cheaper than counseling, so don't be afraid to spend a few bucks to connect regularly with your man.

Notice Today:

What kinds of things does your husband like to do on a date?

Nurture Today:

Pick one of the ideas in this chapter and invite your husband out for a fun and memorable date night. Put it on the calendar today.

He Time, She Time

If the whole body were an ear, where would the sense of smell be?
1 Corinthians 12:17

There we were in the fairy-tale ski town of Lofer, Austria, on the Christmas vacation of a lifetime. I fully expected James to take advantage of the ski slopes while I strolled around the quaint streets and shops. But James would not hear of it. We would ski together. Did I mention I had never skied before in my life? Austria wasn't exactly my idea of the bunny slope. James coached me the night before on the basics of skiing and started calling me Suzy Chapstick.

That beautiful day on the slopes was the low point of our marriage. I fell over and over and over again. And James told me to get up, get up, *get up* over and over again. I sat in the snow begging him to go ski and let me hobble to the snack shop. Oh no, he declared, we were going to stick it out together. To the ski lift.

I've never been more scared in my life. Terrified, I jumped off that lift and careened down that mountain at Mach speed. I turned, turned, turned and actually made it all the way down the slope without falling. Thrilled, James came behind me and said, "Baby, you've got it!" I whipped around shaking. "I couldn't stop. I was totally out of control." My eyes were as wide as saucers. This time, he knew my skiing day was over.

My absolute happiest moment was heading down the mountain in a cable car alone. A few times I could see James in his puffy blue jacket skiing down the mountain. This is how it was meant to be: James skiing the stunning mountains of Austria and me *watching* him ski the stunning mountains of Austria.

Not everything in life has to be shared together.

No doubt, when possible, you want to be your husband's activity buddy. When he thinks of his fondest memories of cycling, fishing, golfing, camping, snorkeling, or whatever, it would be great if you were in a few of those memories. More power to you if you can learn a new skill such as playing tennis because he likes tennis.

My friends Bob and Brenda like boating and RV camping, shooting, and motorcycling. She doesn't scuba dive but she does snorkel. Bob says, "She's a tomboy and classy lady all rolled up in one. It means a lot to me for her to share activities with me whether it's a hike or whatever. I eat up quality time stuff with her."[3]

Bob Lepine, host of *Family Life Today*, remembers when his friends Tim and Darcy Kimmel first got married.

> Tim talks about the fact that when they were dating, one thing he appreciated about Darcy was how much she loved football. Well, she loved being with Tim and Tim loved football, so she loved football. Now after they got married, he would watch his football game and she would go do something else.
>
> On the other hand, Darcy was amazed that Tim liked helping her cut out sewing patterns when they were dating. Well, he didn't really like cutting out patterns and has never done that since they got married. So there's this unrealistic expectation that all these habits will carry over and stay with us. But we can still find those things that we like doing together.[4]

To the Final Four

What if you can't quite get up to speed with your husband's extreme sports, deep-sea fishing trips, or love for ESPN? You can agree peaceably on he time/she time and decide together if either spouse is overdosing on alone time.

Almost twenty-five years ago, I was sitting in Chris Grace's introduction to psychology class at Biola University. A favorite among all the students, Chris and his wife, Alisa, epitomized what we freshman girls wanted: a happy marriage. Dr. Grace still teaches at Biola and serves as the vice president for student development and university planning. Alisa knows what activities Chris loves and needs to rejuvenate himself—watching and playing sports. Chris says,

We are committed as a couple to paying attention to and detecting each other's "dreams"—big and small—then helping the other achieve them. Going to an event like a Dodger or Laker game or the Final Four is not as fun for her, but she knows it allows me to connect with other guy friends and enjoy a game. She wants me to have that experience. I had been to a Final Four before, but was hesitant about going again. I was not sure if I could afford the four days off from work and family. I asked Alisa what she thought, and she strongly encouraged me to go.

Highlights of the trip included getting cheap tickets, serendipitously meeting up with some old friends at the stadium, sleeping in crummy, cheap hotels, and eating at hole-in-the-wall restaurants that I would probably never take Alisa to.

She knows that I "need" to have time away from a busy, everyday world, to hang out and have fun, with no other responsibilities. Such activities often rejuvenate my soul. Alisa knows that I am a better husband and father when I am emotionally and physically recharged, when I spend time and connect with friends, and that I do not often have such opportunities in my busy life and work schedule.

I know she values that which I value, that she pays attention to my dreams and wants me to realize them. That is one aspect of her love for me. I get to go on a very fun trip and I get to do this guilt free, because I know she puts my well-being as a priority. This is her part of her equation for a happy husband, and of course it motivates me to also look for ways to help her achieve her dreams as well.[5]

Is there a dream or activity your husband would like to pursue—big or small—that needs your blessing? If your husband loves restoring cars, you don't want to give him the guilt trip every time he heads to the garage. But you also don't want to feel like you're the fifth wheel and that the old Corvette's getting more love than you. Talk to your husband about making the most of time spent together and time spent apart.

My friend Vickie had a different experience than I did on the ski slopes. She gave it a good college try and then let her husband, Larry, and son hit the slopes, skiing and snowboarding while she read happily in the lodge.

Larry and Vickie keep a good rhythm of he time/she time without keeping score. Larry says,

> Vic has always been active in her professional association, so we adjusted as a family to make it possible for her to attend yearly conventions, which meant I was a single parent for about a week every year. So when I went off with my friends surfing or snowboarding, she became the single parent. We tried to balance each other's interests with neither one getting everything and the other nothing. But no one kept score. It was always, how can we each be happy and be happy together?[6]

You also want to set aside time for you to be with girlfriends and your husband to be with guy friends. It's easy to put this off, especially during the child-raising years, but Tim Hawkins says it's so important:

> I think women worship their kids. They're not doing anyone any favors. They don't have any friends. It's not good. You lose part of who you really are if you're so busy with your kids that you don't have at least one or two consistent relationships with a peer. It's not good for your hubby. I have seen husbands beaten down. If the only adult person in a woman's life is the husband, he just can't do it. He doesn't have the tools for conversation. If he can't do it, where does that leave you? Then the wife feels like the most undesirable, worthless human being, and there goes the self-esteem. There goes the bedroom. There goes everything. So get some friends.[7]

Notice Today:

What are some interests your husband enjoys that you do not? What are interests you both have in common?

Nurture Today:

Plan a fun activity together from the list above. Cut him slack to do his thing once in a while, and you call a girlfriend to have coffee this month.

Day 29

It's Supposed to Be Fun

He will yet fill your mouth with laughter
and your lips with shouts of joy.

JOB 8:21

When James and I were engaged, we met with our wedding coordinator at the church. There just happened to be a wedding scheduled to begin while we were there. After our meeting, we were walking through the lobby and noticed the wedding party getting ready to begin the procession.

James pushed me over to a side door, pretending he was a spy, and said, "Okay, we've got visual contact with the bride. Let's get ready to roll." He crouched at the side door, took out his imaginary gun, and pretty much acted out a scene from *Mission: Impossible*.

I was horrified and said in the most serious voice I could muster, "Sweetheart, this is not funny. This is someone's wedding. Let's leave quietly."

"Get down, hide, they're coming!" James exclaimed, running to another side door.

I just wanted to get in the car and drive away.

That moment didn't play out well for us. We both left the church (that we soon would be married in) upset. He was wondering, *Why is she such a killjoy?* I was thinking, *I can't believe he is so inappropriate.*

I believe this tension exists in many marriages today. Why can't *he* be more serious? Why can't *she* be more fun? (Or vice versa.)

Laugh with Your Husband

Notice I didn't say laugh *at* him. When you constantly laugh together, that fun will carry you through the mundane moments of marriage. The Mayo Clinic says laughter may have the following long-term effects:

- *Improve your immune system.* Positive thoughts actually release neuropeptides that help fight stress and potentially more serious illnesses.

- *Relieve pain.* Laughter may ease pain by causing the body to produce its own natural painkillers. Laughter may also break the pain-spasm cycle common to some muscle disorders.

- *Increase personal satisfaction.* Laughter can also make it easier to cope with difficult situations. It also helps you connect with other people.[8]

Now let's look at these medical benefits through the lens of *marriage* benefits.

- *Improve your immune system.* When you have fun with your spouse, you're less susceptible to infidelity, arguments, or the seven-year itch.

- *Relieve pain.* Laughter can bring down walls between you and your husband in an instant. It breaks the pain cycle of hurting one another and introduces healing instead.

- *Increase personal satisfaction.* Laughter puts oil on the squeaky hinges, making everything in your relationship run smoother, allowing you to better enjoy being married.

Left to my own devices, my idea of fun would be writing books and planning my next talk to a women's group. I'm thankful I enjoy what I do, but this task-oriented mama's got to learn to have more fun.

Just yesterday I was planning to stay home to write this chapter while my husband took the kids to the beach. He asked what I would be writing about. "Having fun," I answered flatly. The irony was painfully obvious. A few minutes later, I was putting on my swimsuit and heading for the beach.

It sounds like an oxymoron, but you can actually learn how to have more fun in your life. Just like a great birthday party doesn't automatically happen (happiness is often planned), you can intentionally put more fun in your marriage.

Tape a funny comic strip or photo on his bathroom mirror. When you see a funny comic strip, take a moment to cut it out for your husband. Find an old photo of a funny memory and put it where your husband will stumble on it.

Watch a funny movie or TV show. Our friend Tim loves old episodes of the *Andy Griffith Show.* James and I love watching episodes with him because Tim's reactions are even funnier than the show itself.

Pull out the joke book. Here's one James and my dad like in common: "A man said to his wife one day, 'I don't know how you can be so stupid and so beautiful all at the same time.' The wife responded, 'Allow me to explain. God made me beautiful so you would be attracted to me; God made me stupid so I would be attracted to you.'"[9]

Learn to laugh at yourselves (see joke above). Today I laugh about James's impersonation of a super spy at that wedding. I didn't find it funny then, but I do now. What if we could learn to laugh at ourselves in the moment?

Play and connect throughout the day. Bob Lepine and his wife, Mary Ann, play word games online. "It helps us keep connected," Bob says. "We're playing a game together in our spare moments, and then we're laughing with each other. 'You scored 107 points on me with that word. I might as well give up now.'"[10]

Bring Back the Fun

When we were dating, I used to do mini-plays for James whenever we passed an empty stage. We could be in a park with an open-air amphitheater, and I'd jump on stage, pretending to be a damsel in distress or a mad scientist. He'd sit back and laugh.

"Why don't you do any more shows?" he asks me now.

"My plays aren't as funny anymore," I reply (though I've made a few lame attempts through the years). "When we were dating, you were so enamored with me, anything I did you thought was hilarious."

"Not so," he says. "Back then, you weren't so reserved."

There's something about marriage that domesticates a couple. I hate to admit my pleas for appropriate behavior have turned my wild lion of a husband into a domesticated cat. Does this scenario painted in *Kiss Me Like You Mean It* sound familiar?

> When you go out together on a "date," it's not romantic. It's not playful. It's not a time of fun and laughter. You're going through the motions. It's a good idea to go out on dates, so that's what you're doing.

"We had a nice time," you say. A date is not supposed to be a "nice time." You have a "nice time" with your mother, or your Aunt Bertha. A real date with your spouse ought to be fun, stimulating, romantic and sensual. That's why you got married.[11]

Here's Clarke's answer to the boring date and ho-hum love life:

The activity alone should never be the focus. The focus is the unpredictable fun, laughter, chemistry, intimacy, and sexual desire you create during the activity...Love is the *greatest*, and nothing could be more serious. But the physical and emotional expression of love between lovers is *not* serious. Love is fun. Love is a blast.[12]

Would your husband describe you as fun? I realize I need to nurture my husband's wild, mischievous side more often to allow James to be fully James. He's toned down through the years to accommodate me. I need to ramp up the fun and loosen up to bless him. When James thinks of a fun person to be with, I want him to think of me. I have a feeling you want the same thing. It's time to turn our homes into places where super spies are free to run.

Notice Today:

What does your husband like to do for fun? What makes him laugh?

Nurture Today:

Encourage your husband to do something that makes him laugh. Pull up a funny video on the computer and leave it open for him (try comedian Tim Hawkins or ventriloquist Mark Thompson for starters).

Day 30

Unstuck

"Forget the former things;
do not dwell on the past.
See, I am doing a new thing."

Isaiah 43:18-19

At a weekend-long writers' conference, I used the restroom several times. There were about fifteen stalls to choose from, and which one do you suppose I chose? I picked the fifth stall every time. Not because it was the only one available, but because I am a creature of habit.

Why are people so drawn to routine? Same row at church, same TV show, same take-out food. Perhaps it's the comfort of the familiar or the fear of the unknown. Maybe we're just too plain lazy to put out the effort to try something new. When this happens in our marriage, we quickly find ourselves in a rut that, if we're not careful, becomes the new normal.

It's time to get unstuck.

Willing to Change

As you may remember, I'm not a camper. During our family's camping trip to Kings Canyon National Park in California, I remember muttering under my breath about wanting to vacation elsewhere as I trudged to the restroom in the middle of the night. I prayed to God for wisdom, and He helped me see beyond my inconvenience.

I realized if I rained on the camping parade, it would ruin the memory of the vacation for my husband and three children. Why would I want to sabotage their happiness? James and the kids *loved* camping. Why couldn't I learn to love camping? James had already made concessions for me. We were in a clean cabin instead of our mini-tent.

I decided to change my attitude. I ended up having a blast walking the Grant Grove trail of the giant sequoias, going under the Tunnel Tree, and climbing the four hundred steps to the peak of Moro Rock with James and the kids. This camping thing was actually turning out to be fun.

In addition to family vacations, you and your spouse need a change of scenery without the kids. David Frisbie says,

> You always benefit from a change of pace. You benefit from being in a place where you can't work and there aren't ten projects calling your name that you should be doing right now because they are more important than idle recreation.
>
> The change of pace aspect is huge. Getting some distance away from your normal life, even if it's half an hour away in the mountains or twenty minutes to the beach, is extremely helpful. While you have the kids at home, if you have relatives or friends who can take them for a weekend or Friday overnight once in a while, you are certainly not rejecting your children to give them to someone's loving care for the weekend. If you can afford it, get a motel. There's nothing unseductive about the home. It's just, especially if you work at home, everything you need to do and ought to do is right in front of you.[13]

My friends Ed and Edie took a Princess Cruise Lines vacation to Alaska and testified that the cruise lived up to its motto, "escape completely." They indeed experienced complete escape aboard that luxurious ship.

You may not be boarding a cruise anytime soon, but what can you do locally to escape completely? How about renting a boat on the lake for a few hours? Going on a mini road trip to a location two hours away? Part of getting unstuck is seeing your spouse in a totally different environment.

Rev It Up

Andy Freeman certainly saw his wife, Teresa, in many different environments during their cross-country motorcycle trip from Phoenix, Arizona, to Asheville, North Carolina. The story of how Teresa got on the bike is as endearing as the trip itself.[14]

The couple lived in North Carolina, but God had opened the door for Andy to do freelance work in Phoenix that turned into two years' worth of contracts. The downside was that for a fourteen-month period, Andy was working in Phoenix for forty-five to fifty days at a time while Teresa was in Charlotte. When a transition occurred at the company, the Lord opened the door for Andy to work back on the East Coast.

Andy had forty days until he started his new job, so he thought about motorcycling across the country. Small detail—he didn't know how to ride a motorcycle yet. He had wanted to ride since he was sixteen, so at age fifty-five, he went to motorcycle school. Andy's plan was to surprise Teresa by riding to her or, even better, inviting her along. He did the latter and she said yes.

The first day, they were scheduled to leave Phoenix in the afternoon for a leisurely ride through the mountain pass to end up at an iconic stucco-teepee hotel on Route 66. Instead, the last check on the motorcycle went awry, and hours later the mechanic was finally getting the headlamp to light. Andy and Teresa finally hit the road at 6:15 p.m. Their first stop was the gas station. As they slowly pulled up to the pump, Andy put his foot down. Someone had spilled some gasoline, so when Andy put his boot down, out went his leg and down went the bike.

"I laid the bike down in slow motion with my wife on the back in front of all these people," Andy remembers.

A man and woman ran over to help them lift the 850-pound bike. Andy and Teresa were first embarrassed, but then they laughed so hard at their first motorcycle accident that happened at the 7-Eleven.

Then Teresa accidently dropped Andy's helmet, and the visor went flying off. She quickly fixed it, but then the headlight went out again. They found the right fuses and finally got on the road.

"Our first hour and half on that bike," Andy says, "we kept saying, we can't have a worse day than this."

They woke up the next day to three solid days of wind gusts of fifty miles an hour.

"Riding a bike is physically not like riding in a car, especially in wind gusts. We were so sore the next day. It felt like someone beat us with a baseball bat. Teresa said, 'What were you thinking wanting to do this?'"

Eight days and three thousand miles later, Andy and Teresa rode into town triumphant. Andy, who had bruises in the shape of handprints on his ribs, said:

Humans are too much like trail horses: I drive to work this way. I stop here for my coffee. I make this sandwich. We start to do that as couples and that's a terrible thing because the one great thing about dating and marriage is all of the excitement and spark, the fireworks. We have stories we're still telling. That motorcycle trip ended over a month ago, and we're still telling people about it.

Getting unstuck can be uncomfortable (think 50 mph wind gusts on a motorcycle), but it sure makes for some great stories. What new chapter can you begin with your husband this month?

Notice Today:

Are you and your husband stuck in a rut in some area of your married life?

Nurture Today:

What is one thing you could do to get unstuck? What can you do this week to add something new to your relationship?

Day 31

To the Eiffel Tower

Being confident of this, that he who began a good work in you
will carry it on to completion until the day of Christ Jesus.

PHILIPPIANS 1:6

Picture your marriage as a photo album. As you open the front cover, what pictures would you find inside?

- Your wedding day
- Dining out on your honeymoon
- Your first apartment
- The birth of your children
- Vacations
- Moving across country in a U-Haul truck

Pause for a moment. What have been your marriage highlights in the past year? The past five years? The past ten? For some of you, the past twenty-five or fifty years? What happy memories jump out at you?

I think of our first apartment on the fourth floor with no elevator in hot Dallas, Texas. We hung black plastic garbage bags that served as drapes for months. They started as a joke, and then we found them to be effective. All we needed was love.

I remember walking in Salzburg, Austria, at Christmastime and seeing the biggest pretzels I've ever laid eyes on. I can picture the tiny hotel room we stayed in. If you stretched your arms out like you were flying, you could almost touch both side walls.

I can see James coming down the stairwell, holding our eight-pound baby boy high in the air, presenting him to the group as if he were Simba from *The Lion King*.

I laugh at how James drove a compact rental car through the most obscure, pot-holed dirt path, lined by sugar cane, in Maui. Yes, the path was on the GPS.

It's heartwarming to picture your married life in snapshot form. To visit each year in your mind. To see the images and hear the laughter. Sure, many of those years have equally dark times, but when you focus on the highlights, I think you're likely to conclude you're married to a pretty great guy.

The Train to Paris

Mary Ann Cole has been married to a pretty great guy for fifty-eight years. Her husband, Glen Cole, was my senior pastor at Capital Christian Center in Sacramento when I was growing up. What a joy to connect again after many years and ask about their secret to growing deeper in love decade after decade. Pastor Cole said,

> When we were looking to be married, things that today are so important we didn't even think about then. A home? A long-term job? (He laughs.) We based ours on love. If that was deep enough, all the rest would fall into place. When I think back about how we started, I'm amazed. I'm not sure I would want it differently. Today's situation is based upon a security with *things*, tangible things. And the intangibles are so often missing.[15]

For Pastor Cole, a happy marriage of fifty-eight years is so normal. But through the reaction of other people, he's reminded that it's special.

Fifty-eight years? You gotta be kidding! And you look so happy!

He answers, "Well, why shouldn't we be? We've worked hard. God has been very good to us."

Did he say "work"? Doesn't a great marriage just happen when two people fall in love?

> You know, when we were kids, we used to say, "I can hardly wait." And we lose that as we get older. But now I've got more "I can hardly waits" than ever. You have to develop high points.

If marriages and families don't have this, life can become pretty much drudgery and a burden. There's such a lack of creativity to make life and marriage what it should be—to keep the cutting edge.

When we lived in the Northwest, we went to the Space Needle in Seattle for our anniversary. That was a highlight—we always looked forward to that. In every area there's something that's special.[16]

To celebrate their latest anniversary, the Coles dined inside the Eiffel Tower to mark the special day. Pastor Cole was scheduled to teach in Brussels on that weekend, so he thought, *Why not make this something to remember until you die?*

I arranged for us to take the bullet train from Brussels to Paris, which is one hour and twenty minutes. At the Eiffel Tower, you take a special elevator right up to the top, above the observation deck. I made these reservations over the Internet. We had a window table and could look out over Paris. It's a pretty special thing to be able to go there on a special day. Once in a while you get the Eiffel Tower experience.[17]

How would you like to be married for fifty plus years and head for the Eiffel Tower to celebrate? Sign me up. Couples today need the hope of the Eiffel Tower. Being married for life isn't a death sentence; it's a life sentence.

It Doesn't Take Money, It Just Takes Thought

You might think, *If I had money to go to Paris, Hawaii, or even a neighboring city, I'd be happy too.* But money isn't required to create a special moment. One tradition that Pastor Cole has is being the first person to call family members on their birthdays. He recalls that his granddaughter wrote in a book of memories on his seventy-fifth birthday, "I never set my alarm the night before my birthday because I know you will call."

Those are memories you can't buy. Pastor Cole says it doesn't take a lot of money, it just takes thought. These are the things that your spouse and children will remember.

James writes me notes on an extremely practical piece of lined 8½ by 11 paper. He cuts out horizontal strips and folds them up. Then he puts them in places for me to find: the back pocket in my jeans, box of tampons (really), in a shoe, in my Bible. These love notes of appreciation pop up everywhere. They didn't cost much money, but they did cost James some time and creativity and thought. Do you think it was worth the cost? Absolutely.

Friend, you and I have been journeying together for thirty-one days on a mission to better love our husbands. Has it been worth the cost for you? Your husband may exclaim, "Absolutely!" And even if he doesn't (yet), know that your heavenly Father says, "Absolutely."

The effort to sweeten a marriage is always worth it. Look ahead and keep the Eiffel Tower in view.

Notice Today:

What is something your husband is looking forward to doing with you in the future?

Nurture Today:

Picture your life ten years from now. How old are you? How old is your husband? How old are your kids? What is your relationship like with your husband? What wonderful experiences do you hope to have with him in the next decade? Jot your dreams down, and then share them with your husband.

Conclusion

Now Let's Talk About Me

"I don't mean to sound selfish,
but can we get back to the subject of 'me?'"

SAM KECKLER

When I saw this tongue-in-cheek quote from Sam, I had to laugh. Doesn't it express what we all feel inside? For thirty-one days, you've been learning about what you can do to bless your husband. As we close this journey together, it's time to talk about you.

You are extremely powerful. I asked a group of professional men, "You are leaders at work making tough decisions and saying hard things to other coworkers and subordinates. Why don't you just tell your wife when you have an unmet need in your life?" The answer was so funny. "We can get another job." In other words, men can't get new wives, so they better not make waves with us. Isn't it funny, ladies, that though our spouses are usually bigger and stronger than we are, they are scared of us?

You have incredible power to change the tone of your marriage. You have the inside guide in your hands. When you recognize your profound influence and choose to use it for good, your home will never be the same. Be open to what your husband says about sex, money, activities, and parenting. You want to get to the point where he's not afraid to tell you anything. You don't want to be intimidating. You want to be inviting.

You are not a quitter. Has your husband changed at all since you started reading and implementing this book? Perhaps a better question is, have you changed? If your husband didn't turn into your dreamboat by Day 15, don't be discouraged. Think of a beautiful mansion overlooking the ocean.

That home didn't just happen in a blink. It started with a blueprint and hour upon hour of meticulous labor. Was it worth it? You bet.

You're building a dream mansion in your marriage. If you stick with the guide for marriage found in the Bible and keep building day after day, you will enjoy the comfort of living in a luxurious, comfortable, rich marriage. Never stop believing that your dream marriage is possible.

You are the woman of his dreams. Do you ever compare yourself to other women? Of course you do. When you see someone more beautiful, you feel like a loser. Guess what? Your husband didn't marry that girl, he married you. He chose you. You were and are the woman of his dreams. You are your husband's big catch. Act like it.

How Writing This Book Has Changed My Marriage

The running joke in my house is James asking, "Now when do these thirty-one days start?" I tell him, "After I finish writing the book on the subject."

When I'd hang up the phone after interviewing someone like Bill Farrel, Cliff and Joyce Penner, or Dave Carder, I'd yell to James, "Oh, you're gonna love what they told me." You see, James could say something until he was blue in the face and I kind of got it. But when expert after expert reinforced the same messages James had been giving me for years, the light went on for me. There's something about receiving advice from a third-party guide that makes it all click. I hope you have found that true for you too.

James and I have been kissing for at least ten seconds a day. The daily peck has turned into something more intimate and sweet between us. Our two-year-old daughter, Lucy, has seen us really kiss for the first time. I'm more excited to schedule and anticipate sex with James. Instead of sex feeling like a duty, it's a decision I now make happily to stay connected and close to my husband. I've loosened up to have more fun. I've reached new physical goals to stay in shape. We've created a new normal that is making both of us much happier in our marriage.

I'm noticing a whole lot more about James these days. My "noticer" has been activated. For instance, one morning I was running late for a women's breakfast. James had gone to the gym extra early so I could go to the breakfast, pulled the car in the driveway facing out, and got my laptop ready for me in the car. As I zipped across town, I had to smile as I noticed all the things he had done for me that morning out of consideration.

As for James, he says the book has been a godsend (and this from a man who has sacrificed a great deal of time and energy so I could write). He says,

> It would have taken us years to figure this out on our own. Many times husbands have an unspoken need, and they just don't know how to put it into words. This book has been a huge time-saver, a huge grief saver. Every couple has the tendency to drift, especially when kids are added into the picture. This book has helped us keep on track and saved us a lot of heartache.

Walking Forward from This Day

I sprained my ankle at the beginning of writing this book. After four months, it was still swollen and sore after walking just a short distance. I babied my foot, fearing maybe a torn ligament or something requiring surgery. Even with our insurance, the copayment alone for an MRI was seven hundred dollars—ouch. But I decided to get it done because I couldn't help but think something was wrong. The MRI showed my ankle was fine and that I just needed to strengthen it through exercise and walking. Before the MRI, I would stop at the first sign of discomfort. Once I knew my ankle was fine, I just kept walking. Now I don't have to push through the pain anymore. My ankle is better.

Your marriage can be like my ankle. Sometimes you worry that something serious is wrong with you and your husband. You wonder if you should back off. At the first sign of stress, you want to stop trying. The Great Physician says your marriage checks out. You've had the MRI and you're a match. There are no relational fractures that can't be healed and redeemed. It may cost some money to see a marriage counselor, go on a second honeymoon, or have date nights, but the investment is certainly worth it. We plunk down money for sports and shoes. Aren't our marriages far more important?

Keep walking forward in the principles that have been guiding you the last thirty-one days. Push through obstacles to get closer to your man. To help you, I've created the "Daily Affirmations of the Happy Wife" on pages 179-180. Read these affirmations out loud for the next thirty-one days to cement these attitudes in your mind and heart. Rip the page right out of the book (I'm giving you permission), make a copy, or retype it. Customize it to fit your needs. Tape it on your bathroom mirror and say it each morning extra loud so your husband can hear you.

Galatians 6:9 says, "Let us not become weary in doing good, for at the proper time we will reap a harvest if we do not give up." Notice it doesn't say to not become weary in "*feeling* good" or "*thinking* good." It says "*doing* good." Our intentions must translate into actions. Remember the DREAM:

> **D**omestic Tranquillity—*Your husband needs a peaceful haven.*
>
> **R**espect—*Your husband needs to be honored in his own home.*
>
> **E**ros—*Your husband needs a fulfilling sex life.*
>
> **A**ttraction—*Your husband needs to be attracted to you.*
>
> **M**utual Activities—*Your husband needs to have fun with you.*

Listen. Do you hear that sound? The band is getting ready to play. Your wedding reception is about to begin. You and your husband have been magically transported to your first moments as newlyweds. You step out on the dance floor, lock eyes, and start to sway.

That reception may have happened a long time ago, but that same man is waiting for you. It's time to dance again.

Daily Affirmations of the Happy Wife

I, _____, am a happy, godly, attractive, and sexy wife. I provide a peaceful and pleasant haven for my husband to come home to. I respect my husband's opinions and recognize him as the leader of our home. I always speak well of my husband to others and look for specific ways to compliment his fine character and behavior. I enjoy having sex with my husband. I crave intimacy with him and want to be uninhibited and free in our lovemaking together. I care about my appearance and take effort to look attractive and to stay fit. I am a fun person who loves to laugh.

Here are some expanded affirmations so you can customize your affirmation by emphasizing the areas you need encouragement in:

Domestic Tranquillity

My home is neat and orderly. I dispose of clutter and take pride in my environment. I am a positive thinker in a negative world. I am happy to be a refuge for my spouse. I am content with what I have and am not obsessed with obtaining material possessions.

Respect

It is my joy to submit to my husband as a way to honor God. Even if my husband doesn't respond the way I'd like, I will respect him and be loyal to him. I will walk in his shoes and seek to understand his perspective.

His preferences are important to me. I will be quick to listen and slow to speak.

Eros

I am intensely sexual. God created me as a sexual being, and I am committed to being intimate with my husband. I am a turned-on woman who's blessed to be with a great guy. I look forward to having great sex this week and can't wait until our next time to express love to each other with freedom.

Attraction

I don't compare myself to airbrushed models or the world's idea of beauty. I am beautiful from the inside out. I am confident in who I am and don't doubt my worth in God's sight. My body is important to me. I strive to maintain a healthy body weight and exercise at least three times a week. I am more attractive to my husband today than the day we were married.

Mutual Activities

I am constantly looking for fun activities to do together with my husband. I don't take myself or life too seriously. I make time for date nights and weekends away to create special memories with my husband. I'm not afraid to try new things. I enjoy my husband's company more than anyone else's.

Notes

Introduction: Are You Still Dreaming?

1. Personal interview with Bob Lepine, July 12, 2011.

Guide 1: Domestic Tranquillity

1. Personal interview with Cindy Hedgecock, June 16, 2011.
2. I recommend Kathi Lipp's *The "What's for Dinner?" Solution* (Eugene, OR: Harvest House Publishers, 2011).
3. Personal interview with John Fuller, July 29, 2011.
4. Personal interview with Tshaka Armstrong, June 14, 2011.
5. Personal interview with David Frisbie, April 8, 2011.
6. "On this Memorial Day," Gypsy Ink blog of Leeana Tankersley, www.gypsyink.com/2011/05/on-this-memorial-day (accessed July 15, 2011).
7. Group interview with Matt Grant, June 19, 2011.
8. Group interview with Derek Malayeri, June 19, 2011.
9. Gary Ezzo and Robert Bucknam, *On Becoming Babywise* (Louisiana, MO: Parent-Wise Solutions, 2006), 22.
10. Personal interview with Mark Matlock, April 13, 2011.
11. Personal interview with Dave Carder, August 24, 2011.
12. Personal interview with Scott Palmer, June 14, 2011.
13. Ibid.
14. Ibid.
15. Ibid.
16. www.brainyquote.com/quotes/authors/n/norman_vincent_peale.html (accessed August 20, 2011).
17. Stories from the Vine, http://storiesfromthevine.com/i-lost-my-job-where-is-god/ (accessed August 15, 2011).
18. Personal interview with John Bias, April 11, 2011.

Guide 2: Respect

1. Matthew Henry, *Matthew Henry's Commentary on the Whole Bible* (Peabody, MA: Hendrickson, 1996), Ephesians 5:21-33.

2. Bruce Wilkinson, quoted from the audio message, "Helper: The Role of the Wife" from *A Biblical Portrait of Marriage* (Atlanta, GA: Walk Thru the Bible, 1995).

3. Personal interview with Glen Cole, June 16, 2011.

4. Personal interview with Bob Lepine, July 12, 2011.

5. Personal interview with David Frisbie, April 8, 2011.

6. Personal interview with Tshaka Armstrong, June 14, 2011.

7. Ibid.

8. Pam Farrel, "Celebrate Spousal Differences," www.crosswalk.com/family/marriage/relationships/celebrate-your-differences.html (accessed August 19, 2011).

9. Personal interview with Tim Hawkins, August 24, 2011.

10. Email interview with Betsy Martin, June 7, 2011.

11. Personal interview with Kevin Sorbo, June 24, 2011.

12. Personal interview with David Clarke, March 28, 2011.

13. David Jeremiah, Turning Point Television, Love at Life Speed broadcast, April 10, 2011.

14. Bruce Wilkinson, audio message "Helper: The Role of the Wife."

15. Personal interview with Curt Hendley, June 26, 2011.

16. Ibid.

17. www.brainyquote.com/quotes/authors/z/zig_ziglar.html (accessed on August 10, 2011).

18. Interview with Tshaka Armstrong.

19. Emerson Eggerichs, Focus on the Family Webcast, www.focusonlinecommunities.com/community/webcasts/2010/1201 (accessed on July 9, 2011).

20. Personal interview with Andy Freeman, June 14, 2011.

21. Personal interview with Mark Matlock, April 13, 2011.

22. Personal interview with Jade Matlock, April 13, 2011.

23. www.imdb.com/title/tt0093779/quotes (accessed on May 17, 2011).

24. Interview with Kevin Sorbo.

25. Ibid.

26. Interview with Mark Matlock.

27. Personal interview with Patrick Brown, April 7, 2011.

Guide 3: Eros

1. Personal interview with David Clarke, March 28, 2011.

2. All quotes from Cliff and Joyce Penner in this chapter are from a personal interview on July 28, 2011.

3. Dennis Prager, "When a Woman Isn't in the Mood: Part 1," www.dennisprager.com/columns.aspx?g=652609e7-f8fe-44d7-834c-7ad9904e41c0&url=when_a_woman_isnt_in_the_mood_part_i (accessed August 22, 2011).

4. Interview with Joyce Penner.

5. Interview with Cliff Penner.

6. www.familysafemedia.com/pornography_statistics.html (accessed August 4, 2011).

7. Personal interview with Sam Keckler, May 6, 2011. You can learn more about his story and ministry at www.samkeckler.com.

8. Ibid.

9. Ibid.

10. Ibid.

11. Interview with Cliff Penner.

12. Personal interview with Dave Carder, August 24, 2011.

13. Personal interview with David Frisbie, April 8, 2011.

14. Personal interview with Bill Farrel, July 22, 2011.

15. Ibid.

16. Interview with Cliff and Joyce Penner.

17. Interview with David Frisbie.

18. Interview with Dave Carder.

19. Interview with David Clarke.

20. Ibid.

21. Ibid.

22. Interview with David Frisbie.

23. Bill and Pam Farrel, *Red-Hot Monogamy* (Eugene, OR: Harvest House Publishers, 2006), 137-38.

24. Interview with Cliff Penner.

25. Linda Dillow and Lorraine Pintus, *Intimate Issues* (Colorado Springs, CO: WaterBrook Press, 1999), 56.

26. Personal interview with Tim Hawkins, August 24, 2011.

27. Leeana Tankersley, *Found Art* (Grand Rapids, MI: Zondervan, 2009), 70-71.

28. Personal interview with Bob Meissner, April 2, 2011.

29. Kevin Leman, *Sex Begins in the Kitchen* (Grand Rapids, MI: Revell, 1999), 9-10.

30. David Clarke, *Kiss Me Like You Mean It* (Grand Rapids, MI: Revell, 2009), 99-102.

31. Interview with David Clarke.

32. Interview with Joyce Penner.

33. Interview with Tim Hawkins.

Guide 4: Attraction

1. Willard Harley, *His Needs, Her Needs* (Grand Rapids, MI: Revell, 1986), 103.

2. For more tips on how to look and feel your best, see my book *31 Days to a Younger You* (Eugene, OR: Harvest House Publishers, 2010).

3. Personal interview with David Jeremiah, July 19, 2011.

4. Personal interview with Patrick Brown, April 7, 2011.

5. Personal email interview with Louis Messer, April 2, 2011.

6. Emerson Eggerichs, Focus on the Family Webcast, www.focusonlinecommunities.com/community/webcasts/2010/1201 (accessed on July 9, 2011).

7. Personal interview with Scott Palmer, June 14, 2011.

8. Matthew Henry, *Matthew Henry's Commentary on the Whole Bible* (Peabody, MA: Hendrickson Publishers, 2008), 1 Peter 3:1-7.

9. Cindi McMenamin, *When a Woman Inspires Her Husband* (Eugene, OR: Harvest House, 2011), 9.

10. Personal interview with David Frisbie, April 8, 2011.

11. Paul Lee Tan, *Encyclopedia of 7700 Illustrations: Signs of the Times*, illustration 2333.

12. Personal interview with Bob Lepine, July 12, 2011.
13. Personal interview with Tim Hawkins, August 24, 2011.
14. Personal interview with John Fuller, July 29, 2011.
15. Ibid.
16. Interview with Patrick Brown.
17. Personal interview with Mary Burger, July 14, 2011.
18. Personal interview with David Clarke, March 28, 2011.
19. Personal interview with Glen Cole, June 16, 2011.
20. McMenamin, *When a Woman Inspires Her Husband*, 160.
21. Personal interview with Mark Matlock, April 13, 2011.
22. Ibid.
23. Personal email interview with Bob Clark, July 7, 2011.
24. Interview with David Jeremiah.
25. Ibid.
26. Ibid.

Guide 5: Mutual Activities
1. Personal interview with Andy Freeman, June 14, 2011.
2. You can find a directory at www.drive-ins.com for drive-in theaters still in operation.
3. Personal interview with Bob Lepine, July 12, 2011.
4. Ibid.
5. Personal email interview with Chris Grace, July 11, 2011.
6. Personal email interview with Larry Pierce, August 3, 2011.
7. Personal interview with Tim Hawkins, August 24, 2011.
8. Mayo Clinic, "Stress Relief from Laughter?" www.mayoclinic.com/health/stress-relief/SR00034 (accessed June 19, 2011).
9. www.romancestuck.com/jokes/marriage-jokes.htm (accessed June 22, 2011).
10. Interview with Bob Lepine.
11. David Clarke, *Kiss Me Like You Mean It* (Grand Rapids, MI: Revell, 2009), 79.
12. Ibid., 80, 97.
13. Personal interview with David Frisbie, April 8, 2011.
14. The story and quotes about this trip are based on my interview with Andy Freeman.
15. Personal interview with Glen Cole, June 16, 2011.
16. Ibid.
17. Ibid.

The Wives of Happy Husbands Club
Discussion Guide

Guide 1: Domestic Tranquillity

Your husband needs a peaceful haven.

Are you domestically challenged or a domestic diva?

Imagine being your husband walking into your house after a day of work. How would you like to be greeted?

What's the environment of your home most days? Is it happy, calm, fun, tense, hurried, or _____?

If you have children, what are some of your husband's strengths as a father?

Do you think your husband knows he is a priority in your life or does he feel he has to take a number to get your attention?

Is money a stress in your relationship? If so, how? What can you do to reduce financial stress for your husband?

Guide 2: Respect

Your husband needs to be honored in his own home.

Do you have trouble submitting to your husband? Why or why not?

Share an example of doing something that you didn't want to do, but you did it out of respect for your husband.

Why do you think it's important to have one leader in the home?

Do you think your husband knows he is loved and accepted as he is? Or is there an area of his life that you are constantly harping on?

If someone followed you around and recorded every single word you said to your husband in one week (not counting the sweet nothings just between you and him), would you be embarrassed?

How often do you disagree and fight? Do you fight fair? How could you offer "a cup of kindness" during your next tiff? (Remember Jade brewing a cup of hot tea for her husband even when she was irritated.)

When you were falling in love with your husband, he was your knight in shining armor. What were a few qualities that drew you to him in the first place?

Guide 3: Eros

Your husband needs a fulfilling sex life.

First Corinthians 7:9 says, "It's better to marry than to burn with passion." Now that your husband is obviously married, do you think he ever feels like he is burning with passion or are his sexual needs lavishly met?

Do you agree that sexual fulfillment is the number one need of your husband? Who desires sex more in your marriage, you or your husband?

What are your roadblocks to intimacy?

When you are sexually disinterested or inhibited, what do you think that communicates to your husband?

Cliff Penner says a wife has the right to be intensely sexual. What are ways you can think about sex more and enjoy it more?

What would lead to a better sex life? Scheduling time? More spontaneity? Weekend getaways?

How can you be a dream lover to your husband?

Guide 4: Attraction

Your husband needs to be attracted to you.

Willard Harley writes, "By calling for a wife to be attractive, I mean she should take pains to look something like the woman her husband married." Do you agree with this statement?

How important do you think your appearance is to your husband?

Are you willing to make some easy and hard changes in your appearance to please your husband? (Easy = wearing his favorite shirt; Hard = losing a dress size)

Does your husband like your sense of style?

What do you wear to bed?

What's your disposition around your husband like on most days? Would you choose yourself as a person you'd want to hang out with?

Do you communicate calmly and clearly to your husband or are you overly dramatic?

Do hard times drive you and your husband apart or closer together?

Guide 5: Mutual Activities

Your husband needs to have fun with you.

What's the most recent fun thing you've done with your husband?

What are three things you enjoy doing together?

When was the last time you went on a date with your husband? How often do you date?

Look at Bob and Jana's twenty-five date ideas in Day 27. Which one would you like to do next?

Share one of the favorite dates you've had with your husband.

When was the last time you and your husband had a really good laugh? What was so funny?

Let's say you and your husband always go to the same place and do the same things. What's one thing you can do to break out of your rut?

What's one thing you dream about doing with your husband in the next ten years?

Acknowledgments

Thank you to all the happy husbands who agreed to be interviewed and quoted for this book. Time and time again, I was amazed at who said yes. The book is so much richer with the insights of:

Not just one Dr. David, but three.

Dr. David Jeremiah—What a blessing you and Donna have been to my family through the years. I have been touched by your upfront ministry and your behind-the-scenes, rock-solid family.

Dr. David Frisbie—You and Lisa have cheered me on every step of the way. Thank you for all your support, advice, and wisdom.

Dr. David Clarke—You exposed the "peck" kiss James and I had gotten used to. Thank you for helping couples put fun back into marriage.

Dr. Cliff and Joyce Penner—Your classic bestseller *The Gift of Sex* helped me when I was first married. Now you've helped me again understand sexuality better. What an honor to include your insights.

Tim Hawkins—I'm so glad we met at Mastermind and that the name-dropping worked. Your hilarious comedy has blessed my family and so many others.

Kevin Sorbo—You have accomplished something heroic in Hollywood by being a happy husband and father. Thank you for living out that example.

Bill Farrel—You and Pam are the poster children for a wonderful marriage. After talking to you, I felt like a light was turned on. You help us (women) get you (men).

Bob Lepine—You speak with such wisdom and grace; no wonder we turn to you and *Family Life Today* for solid biblical advice for the family.

John Fuller—My heart is still touched when I think of you, Dena, and your six children. Your candor and commitment are extremely refreshing. You embody the values of Focus on the Family.

Dave Carder—No wonder God has used you to counsel so many couples. Your tenacity, passion, and insights are remarkable.

Mark Matlock—I am thrilled that after being together at Biola University over two decades ago, we got to connect again. I'm so proud of you and Jade and what you have done to impact youth in America.

Dr. Chris Grace—You and Alisa had the marriage we freshmen girls wanted at

Biola. Decades later you still have that (plus you haven't aged). Thank you for lighting the way for so many couples and students.

Patrick Brown—We think of you often when we see Ethan's room. So glad God had our paths cross. You and Denise have something so special, and we're privileged to get a peek into that in the book.

Scott Palmer—The *Better TV* show was especially exciting in New York City because I got to meet you and Bethany. Thank you for sharing your stories and the money personalities.

Pastor Glen Cole—Sitting under your leadership at Capital Christian Center as a high schooler changed my life. Thank you and Mary Ann for being married fifty-eight years strong and acting like newlyweds.

Tshaka Armstrong—You are using your gift to get dads talking. Thank you for sharing your story of reconciliation that brings hope to others.

Andy Freeman—I'm not sure how many other men would go to motorcycle school in their fifties and then ride across the United States with their wife hanging on for dear life. Thank you for bringing humor, zest, and integrity to all you do.

Sam Keckler—Thank you for addressing the tough topic of pornography with passion and transparency. You and Maria are walking billboards of the power of God to transform and use people. You shine brightly.

Curt Hendley—To the original happy husband blogger, thank you for your kindness and generosity. I appreciate your desire to help couples succeed in marriage.

Bob Meissner—What a joy to meet at your church. The love you and Susan have is much better than fiction.

Bryant Engebretson—I guess I have you to thank for the new bedtime wardrobe? Still waiting for the fireplace to come in…

Doug Hedrick—Thank you for working to strengthen military families. Kudos to Ally for all her creativity. Go Flat Daddy!

Louis Messer—From your month-long honeymoon camping across Canada in 1953 to today, you and Sally make marriage look fun. Thank you for your unwavering commitment to each other and to loving others so generously.
Bob LaFave—You and Jana could get couples dating again with your creative ideas and example. You prioritize your marriage and it shows.

John Bias—Thank you and Trilby for your openness. You shared about the hard topic of unemployment with candor and helped us as wives understand the effect that can have on a husband.

George Burger—It's apparent that you and Mary love each other deeply after sixty plus years of marriage. Your commitment and reliance on prayer and studying God's Word together gives us a model to follow.

Jim Brown—I remember driving home with Diane from a women's retreat and how you greeted her so warmly and got her suitcase from the car. I thought, *Now that's a happy husband*. Go Chargers!

Ed Chapman, Bob Clark, Mike Adams, Derek Malayeri, and all the men in our Parenting with Purpose class—Thank you for letting me pick your brains about what makes a husband happy. I am so blessed by the discussions we have on Sundays.

And of course, the happiest husband of them all (at least in my house), James Pellicane. Pretty much anything interesting or useful in this book originated from a conversation between you and me. I think your funny saying, "You got the questions, I've got the answers," is true. In the writing phase, you were my toughest critic and loudest cheerleader. The book is so much better because of you. Not to mention my life. I love you, sweetheart.

My kids—My prayer is that you'll read this someday and be blessed in your own marriages and understand your funny parents better. Thanks to my accountability partner Ethan, who would continually ask me, "Mom, how many chapters have you written so far?" Thank you, Noelle, for all your hugs and kisses. And thanks even to Lucy, who was mostly distracting but at times would sit quietly on my lap while I typed.

My parents—Ann and Peter Kho and Marilyn and Arthur Pellicane—thank you for believing in me, watching the kids so I could write, and making vacation plans to look forward to.

My Harvest House family—What a joy to work with you. I am touched by your heart to serve God and people through excellent books. Thank you to my editor, Rod Morris, for the wisdom of your experience and your lightning-fast response time to any question.

Lastly, my mentor, Pam Farrel—I wouldn't be writing this book at this time without your help. You helped this turtle get on the fence post. Thank you for investing in me over and over again. You are amazing.

Visit Arlene's website for bonus material.

www.ArlenePellicane.com

- Listen to the interviews of many men featured in the book, such as David Jeremiah and Tim Hawkins.

- Enhance your reading with corresponding video teachings from Arlene.

- Keep the discussions going through the blog.

- Find more creative date ideas.

- Get the encouragement you need to succeed in your marriage.

About Arlene Pellicane

Arlene and her happy husband, James, live in San Diego, California, with their three children, Ethan, Noelle, and Lucy. Arlene is also the author of *31 Days to a Younger You*. Before becoming a stay-at-home mom, Arlene worked as the associate producer for *Turning Point Television* with David Jeremiah as well as a features producer for *The 700 Club*. She received her BA in intercultural studies from Biola University and her master's in journalism from Regent University.

Arlene has appeared as a guest on *The Hour of Power*, *The 700 Club*, *Turning Point with Dr. David Jeremiah*, *Better TV*, and TLC's *Home Made Simple*. An energetic communicator, she shares humorous and compelling stories to guide women to positive life change.

For free resources along with information about contacting Arlene to speak at your event, visit www.ArlenePellicane.com.

31 Days to a Younger You
No Surgery, No Diets, No Kidding

If 40 is the new 30 and 50 is the new 40…how is the average woman supposed to keep up? There's got to be an easier way to look younger than Botox treatments, yo-yo dieting, or plastic surgery.

Arlene Pellicane offers readers a less troublesome (and less expensive!) solution to looking younger and feeling younger in just 31 days, especially for women who want to

- have more energy
- look 5-10 years younger
- be happier and healthier
- lose a dress size or more
- improve their mood and sense of well-being
- prevent illnesses such as diabetes and heart disease

Women of all ages will benefit from Arlene's beauty and health tips, along with her biblical encouragement to "grow more beautiful from the inside out."

> "Arlene has the gift of encouragement.
> She's done what many women want to do.
> She helps you *want* to make good choices!"
>
> —PAM FARREL, AUTHOR OF
> *MEN ARE LIKE WAFFLES—WOMEN ARE LIKE SPAGHETTI*

To learn more about Harvest House books and
to read sample chapters, log on to our website:

www.harvesthousepublishers.com

HARVEST HOUSE PUBLISHERS
EUGENE, OREGON